ROYAL NAVY
TORPEDO-BOMBERS
VS
AXIS WARSHIPS

1939–45

MATTHEW WILLIS

OSPREY PUBLISHING
Bloomsbury Publishing Plc
Kemp House, Chawley Park, Cumnor Hill, Oxford, OX2 9PH, UK
29 Earlsfort Terrace, Dublin 2, Ireland
1385 Broadway, 5th Floor, New York, NY 10018, USA
E-mail; info@ospreypublishing.com
www.ospreypublishing.com

OSPREY is a trademark of Osprey Publishing Ltd

First published in Great Britain in 2022

A catalogue record for this book is available from the British Library.

ISBN: PB 9781472852489; eBook 9781472852458;
ePDF 9781472852472; XML 9781472852465

22 23 24 25 26   10 9 8 7 6 5 4 3 2 1

Edited by Tony Holmes
Cover artworks, battlescene, three-views, cockpit, Engaging the Enemy and
armament artwork by Jim Laurier
Maps and tactical diagrams by www.bounford.com
Index by Angela Hall
Typeset by PDQ Digital Media Solutions, UK
Printed and bound in India by Replika Press Private Ltd

Osprey Publishing supports the Woodland Trust, the UK's leading woodland
conservation charity.

To find out more about our authors and books visit
www.ospreypublishing.com. Here you will find extracts, author interviews,
details of forthcoming events and the option to sign up for our newsletter.

Acknowledgements
Thanks to Dave Long, Andreas Biermann, Enrico Cernuschi, Marcus
Faulkner, Philip Ryley, Brian Ryley, Derrik Armson, 'Bertie' Vigrass, Lynn
Ritger and Navy Wings.

Matapan *Pola* cover art
The critical moment in the Battle of Matapan on 27 March 1941, when Sub
Lt G. P. C. Williams of 829 NAS – probably the last pilot to drop his torpedo
in the final strike of the day – scored a hit on the heavy cruiser *Pola*, bringing
it to a complete stop. The entire Italian force present had assembled a
protective screen around the crippled battleship *Vittorio Veneto*, damaged by an
Albacore earlier in the day. Intense anti-aircraft fire and a smokescreen
prevented the strike from making a combined attack, forcing the ten aircraft to
target ships individually or in small groups. *Pola* was subsequently engaged in
a night action with Royal Navy battleships as a result of the torpedo hit, and it
was sunk along with two more cruisers.

Bismarck cover art
Swordfish from 825 NAS, embarked in HMS *Victorious*, attack the
Kriegsmarine battleship *Bismarck* on the evening of 24 May 1941 – just hours
after it had sunk HMS *Hood*. The squadron was not at full strength and had
not completed training, but the attack was carried out with courage and skill,
scoring one hit on the main armour belt, exacerbating damage from an earlier
shell hit. Despite heavy anti-aircraft fire, no Swordfish were shot down.

Previous page
A Mk XII practice torpedo is fitted to a Swordfish using a standard torpedo
handling trolley. The aircraft's torpedo crutches are visible beneath the
fuselage. (Author's Collection)

CONTENTS

INTRODUCTION

In 1914 the Royal Navy regarded the aeroplane as a useful but peripheral part of its armoury. Soon after the end of World War I, it was a vital aspect of the main battle fleet. From 1918 until the 1950s, the aircraft carrier was central to the Royal Navy's main force, and its chief weapon was the torpedo-bomber.

The dramatic success of the Whitehead self-propelled torpedo in the 1877–78 Russo-Turkish War meant this new 'ship-killing' weapon could not be ignored by any major navy. Methods of delivery soon encompassed small boats, battleships, shore installations and submarines. After the evolution of a practical, controllable, heavier-than-air aeroplane, consideration was given to aircraft delivering torpedo strikes, and in July 1914 Sqn Ldr A. M. Longmore proved the possibility by dropping an 810lb 14in. torpedo from a Short 'Folder' S.64 seaplane. Following this, the Royal Naval Air Service (the predecessor to the Fleet Air Arm) charged Short Brothers with developing a floatplane fully capable of a practical torpedo strike, resulting in the Short Admiralty Type 184. Two early examples were brought to the Aegean in 1916, where they carried out the first successful torpedo attacks on ships by aircraft.

Around the same time, flying-off decks were introduced on seaplane carriers, allowing aircraft with wheeled undercarriages to take off at sea, evolving into the aircraft carrier by 1918. HMS *Furious*, a modified battlecruiser, launched the first successful carrier strike in history with an attack on Zeppelin sheds at Tondern, in Denmark, on 19 July 1918. Before the end of the war, a specialist carrier aircraft for torpedo attack, the Sopwith Cuckoo, had been developed and a squadron formed to target the German High Seas Fleet. The armistice ended this plan, but the carrier-based torpedo-bomber was by then a fixture in the British armoury.

Between the wars, the Fleet Air Arm developed the technology, tactics and strategy that cemented the torpedo-bomber's place in the service. Fleet exercises

Swordfish L7650 of the Torpedo Training Unit, based at Gosport, in Hampshire, demonstrating a perfect torpedo drop in 1938–39. The torpedo is beginning its run just beneath the surface in the direction intended, and it will assume the set depth after a short distance. A torpedo dropped at the wrong height, attitude or while the aircraft was yawing could run incorrectly or break up. (Author's Collection)

proved the vulnerability of a battle fleet to a well-coordinated torpedo attack from aircraft.

In the mid-1930s, the Fleet Air Arm was constrained by small numbers of airframes. As a result, the service began to consolidate its roles across a smaller number of less-specialised types. Dedicated torpedo-bomber, gunnery spotter and reconnaissance machines were therefore replaced with a single Torpedo Spotter Reconnaissance (TSR) aircraft, of which the first in service was the Blackburn Shark in 1934, followed shortly after by the Fairey Swordfish in 1936.

AXIS WARSHIPS

During World War I, Germany and Italy had powerful, modern navies with fleets built around up-to-date dreadnought battleships. In the years before World War II, both nations needed to rebuild and update. In Italy's case, economics and naval treaties prevented new battleship construction. Germany had lost the vast majority of its fleet after World War I and was forced to start from scratch, initially impeded by the Versailles Treaty restrictions. The country had no existing battleships that could be modernised to supplement new builds, unlike Japan, Britain and Italy. Germany was only allowed to build a handful of modern vessels in the 1920s and early 1930s.

The introduction of the Deutschland-class *panzerschiffe* (literally 'armoured ships', known in Britain as 'pocket battleships' due to their heavy-calibre main armament) triggered a naval arms-race among European navies. First, France introduced the Dunkerque-class battlecruisers, which spurred Italy to initiate the Littorio-class

The modernised Italian battleships *Conte di Cavour* (centre) and *Giulio Cesare* (left) in port shortly before Italy's entry into World War II. The modernisation of these vessels dramatically improved their existing performance, fighting strength and protection, although they were still vulnerable to aerial torpedo attack. (Author's Collection)

battleships and Germany to significantly alter its plans. What would have been the fourth and fifth *panzerschiffe* were reworked into larger, faster, more heavily armed and armoured ships that could fight on at least equal terms with the French vessels. Furthermore, Italy embarked on a programme of modernising existing battleships to make them as competitive as possible, improving their speed, protection and armament. The balance of speed and powerful armament of the Deutschland-class (28 knots, six 11in. guns) made high speed a particular priority of the battleships that were created in response.

A similar race took place with cruisers. The typical 'treaty cruiser' of the late 1920s and early 1930s was significantly compromised to stay within mandated tonnage limits, with protection usually the element to suffer most. Cruisers like the British County-class and the French Duquesne-class were lightly armoured by the standards of their 8in. armament. The French vessels in particular emphasised speed, which prompted the Regia Marina to develop the fast, lightly armoured Trento-class.

With the collapse of the naval treaties in the late 1930s, both Italy and Germany were finally free to build warships unhindered by external restrictions – although in truth both had been working on non-treaty compliant designs for some time, allowing for a better balance of performance, protection and armament. These included the Littorio- and Bismarck-class battleships and the Admiral Hipper- and Zara-class heavy cruisers. It would be the fruits of this arms race that the Fleet Air Arm's torpedo-bombers would have to meet in battle.

CHRONOLOGY

1914
28 July

Short 'Folder' S.64 flown by Sqn Ldr A. M. Longmore drops a torpedo into the Solent off Calshot in the first successful torpedo drop by an aeroplane in Britain.

1915
12 August

Flight Commander C. H. K. Edmonds sinks a Turkish ship in the Aegean, the first vessel sunk by an air-dropped torpedo.

1927
11 June

The Reichsmarine decides on the form that its new *panzerschiffe* will take.

1932
26 November

Italian Admirals' Committee considers plans for new battleships or a radical modernisation of Conte di Cavour-class dreadnoughts in response to French Dunkerque-class battlecruisers.

1933
1 March

The Reichsmarine elects to replace the fourth and fifth *panzerschiffe* with a larger and faster design, leading to the Scharnhorst-class.

1934
17 April

First flight of the prototype Fairey TSR II, later known as the Swordfish.

28 October

Battleships *Littorio* and *Vittorio Veneto* are laid down in the Ansaldo and CRDA shipyards, respectively.

1935
18 June

Anglo-German Naval Agreement signed.

16 November

Two Bismarck-class battleships ordered.

1936
27 July

Fleet Air Arm's 825 Naval Air Squadron (NAS) becomes the first frontline unit to receive the Swordfish.

1937
30 September

Blackburn Shark is retired by 821 NAS, making the Swordfish the sole torpedo-bomber in frontline Fleet Air Arm service.

1938
12 December

First flight of the prototype Fairey Albacore, designed to replace the Swordfish in Fleet Air Arm service.

1939
27 January

Führer Adolf Hitler agrees Plan Z, Großdmiral Erich Raeder's proposal for a large conventional surface fleet, including ten battleships and three battlecruisers.

24 May

Royal Navy finally regains control over the Fleet Air Arm from the RAF.

1940

15 March
Albacore enters service with 826 NAS, but will not embark operationally on a fleet carrier for a year.

10 April
Start of Operation *Weserübung*, the German seaborne invasion of Norway.

12–13 November
Battle of Taranto sees three Italian battleships sunk at anchor by Swordfish.

7 December
First flight of the Fairey Barracuda, the Fleet Air Arm's first monoplane torpedo-bomber.

1941

25 February
Tirpitz, the second Bismarck-class battleship, commissioned.

20 March
Aircraft from HMS *Ark Royal* locate *Scharnhorst* and *Gneisenau* during Operation *Berlin*, but lose contact before a strike can be mounted.

27–28 March
During Battle of Cape Matapan, Fleet Air Arm Albacores torpedo and seriously damage *Vittorio Veneto* and *Pola*, putting the former out of action for months and leading to the sinking of the latter, and two other Italian cruisers, by Royal Navy battleships.

24 May
Battle of Denmark Strait. Later, HMS *Victorious'* Swordfish deliver a torpedo attack on *Bismarck*, scoring one hit and exacerbating earlier shell damage.

26 May
HMS *Ark Royal's* Swordfish torpedo *Bismarck*, allowing it to be caught and sunk by Royal Navy warships.

1942

12 February
Six Swordfish of 825 NAS attempt to attack *Scharnhorst*, *Gneisenau* and *Prinz Eugen* in the English Channel, but are shot down.

5 May
Swordfish from 829 NAS sink the Vichy French auxiliary cruiser *Bougainville* with torpedoes in the last such attack made by Swordfish against an enemy surface warship.

1943

31 March
810 NAS, the final fleet torpedo-bomber squadron equipped with Swordfish, exchanges its aircraft for Barracudas.

10 September
Italian battle fleet surrenders to the Royal Navy following the armistice between Italy and the Allies.

30 November
820 NAS, the final fleet torpedo-bomber squadron equipped with Albacores, disbands.

1944

9 May
Barracudas operating from HMS *Furious* attack a convoy and its escort with a mix of torpedoes and bombs off Kristiansund in almost certainly the last Fleet Air Arm torpedo attack against surface ships of the war.

DESIGN AND DEVELOPMENT

In June 1943, Commodore Matthew Slattery, serving as Chief Naval Representative, Ministry of Aircraft Production and Director-General of Naval Aircraft Development and Production, described 'The place assigned to the Fleet Air Arm in the general plans for the Navy', as having the 'main objective of command of the seas. Their biggest problem was the destruction of the enemy fleet. There might be only one chance of interception with an enemy fleet that was seeking to evade action. Therefore, the primary function of the Fleet Air Arm was long-range reconnaissance and spotting

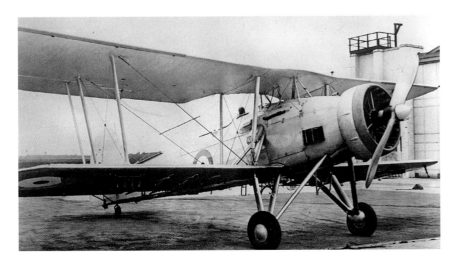

K4190, the prototype TSR II, later known as Swordfish. Although the aircraft is still in its early configuration, with a two-bladed propeller and bulged cowling, it has been fitted with torpedo crutches, six universal bomb carriers and two light-series carriers beneath the wings – the standard fit for Swordfish until 1944, allowing a torpedo or a range of bombs and other stores to be carried. (Author's Collection)

for the Fleet. Their secondary function was, having found the enemy, to reduce his speed by torpedo attack if he should attempt to run away'.

The purpose of the Fleet Air Arm's torpedo-bombers was not, therefore, to sink enemy warships in their own right – achieving this would be unlikely, particularly in the case of battleships. The 18in. Mk XII torpedo was not powerful enough to guarantee sinking a large warship, but even a single hit could slow a vessel down for a period of time by causing flooding or machinery damage. This, along with vital reconnaissance, made the Fleet Air Arm an integral part of the Royal Navy's battle fleet.

The characteristics of the Swordfish, Albacore and Barracuda were dictated by a number of factors. The Admiralty tended to prioritise capability at the expense of performance, and the weapons and equipment that had to be carried were non-negotiable. Aircraft had to fulfil wildly differing functions, and the factor that suffered most tended to be performance. Furthermore, the Admiralty took a conservative approach to deck-landing, requiring low speed and good control down to the stall, as well as excellent visibility for the pilot. It was not until 1940 that the consequences of this approach were realised and steps taken to improve the situation.

The Air Ministry also contributed to the difficulties, as whenever a new aircraft's performance fell short, they would recommend that the specification be withdrawn and a new one prepared. This happened on three occasions from 1927 to 1939, and in each case simply led to more delay rather than a better aeroplane.

The Swordfish was the Fleet Air Arm's main torpedo-bomber from 1937 to 1940, and it remained in the frontline in that role as late as 1942. It was developed from a spotter-reconnaissance aircraft that Fairey Aviation prepared for the stillborn Specification S.9/30, by way of a private-venture development for the Greek Navy. The prototype first flew on 21 March 1933 at Harmondsworth, in Middlesex, but was lost when it crashed on 11 September after the aircraft entered an irrecoverable flat spin. It was then redesigned with some haste to promote spin recovery, with a longer fuselage, larger tail surfaces and greater wing sweepback.

The resulting TSR II found favour with the testing establishments and was ordered, with the name Swordfish, entering service in 1936. The Fleet Air Arm's torpedo-bomber squadrons had standardised on the Swordfish by the end of that year. Few alterations were made to the Swordfish's design during its period as the main Fleet Air Arm torpedo-bomber, the most significant modification being the introduction of Air-to-Surface Vessel (ASV) Mk II radar in early 1941.

The rapid advancement of aircraft design meant that consideration of the Swordfish's replacement was already in hand by the time it was in widespread service. The primacy of the monoplane was clear, but the Air Ministry advised the Admiralty not to switch directly to such a design, but adopt a biplane with more advanced features in the interim. The resulting aircraft was the Albacore, which was

SWORDFISH I

35ft 8in.

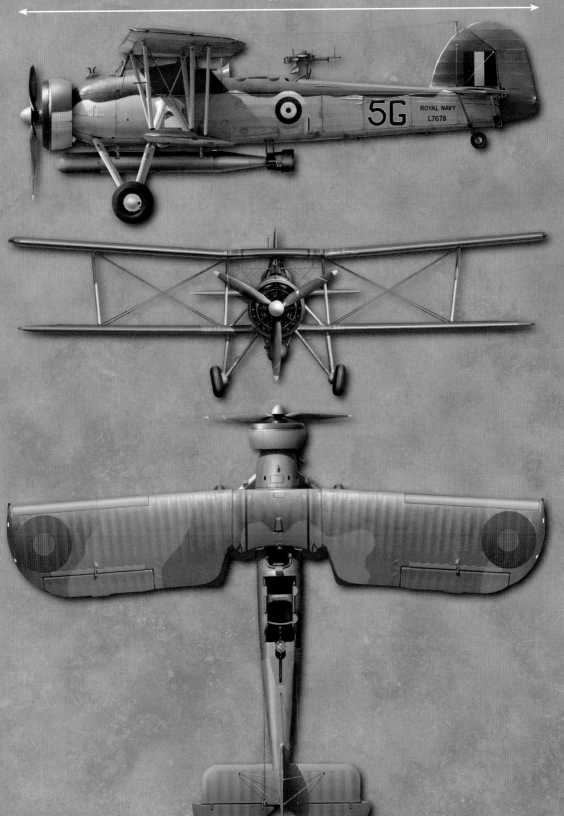

12ft 4in.

45ft 6in.

The Albacore was intended as a short-term replacement for the Swordfish and a stepping-stone to a more advanced monoplane. Note the torpedo carried by the aircraft has its undersides painted black. The Albacore often operated at night, and this practice prevented reflections off the metal body. (Author's Collection)

The Barracuda was the aircraft intended to fully supplant the Swordfish, which it did on its much-delayed entry into service in late 1943. This early-production example (P9667) is demonstrating the use of the Fairey-Youngman flaps as dive brakes to permit a steep dive to torpedo-dropping altitude, enabling the aircraft to make its initial approach out of the range of anti-aircraft batteries. (Author's Collection)

described by some Fleet Air Arm personnel as a 'gentleman's Swordfish'. It had a useful increase in speed and range, and improved crew comfort, when compared to its predecessor, but the Albacore's performance was still significantly below even the least impressive monoplanes of the same class, such as the Douglas TBD Devastator.

At the outbreak of war, the Fleet Air Arm was faced with a difficult situation, as the Swordfish was about to end production, but Albacore production had not yet got up to speed. Blackburn had been approached to discuss it also commencing the construction of Albacores, but potential losses in wartime meant that the Fleet Air Arm might run out of aircraft before the new supply was available. One solution was for Blackburn to take over Swordfish production instead, using the jigs and tools that were already in use by Fairey but which would be surplus to requirements when the company switched to Albacore production.

If the Albacore was intended to help the Fleet Air Arm transition to a more modern successor while serving only briefly in the frontline, it failed. Indeed, the only developments likely to acclimatise crews to newer technology were hydraulic flaps and a variable pitch propeller. Other innovations such as a retractable undercarriage, dive brakes and a modern torpedo fire-control system would have to wait until the Barracuda was introduced from late 1942. When this took place, there were numerous losses attributed to crews being unused to the characteristics of a monoplane. The Albacore did, however, provide the Fleet Air Arm with a useful increase in performance and range in 1941–42, which were of benefit in the Mediterranean against fast Italian warships.

The Albacore was only ever considered a short-term replacement for the Swordfish, and the aircraft intended to supplant it comprehensively was the Barracuda. This aeroplane was conceived in 1937 as a result of Specification S.24/37 for a TSR with a cruising speed of 212mph, a stalling speed of no more than 67mph, and a range of 690 miles. Although all the designs submitted were monoplanes, the preferred Fairey Type 100 was the only one with a retractable undercarriage.

An order was placed in January 1939, with the aircraft expected to enter service in 1941. However, the selected engine was cancelled in August 1939, and time was lost choosing a replacement and redesigning the airframe to accept it. In May 1940, the Ministry of Aircraft Production decreed that priority for resources was to be given to five aircraft, none of them Fleet Air Arm types, virtually stopping development of the Barracuda. A change of Chief Designer and widespread mismanagement at Fairey caused additional delays.

Furthermore, the Barracuda was simply a much more complex design than its predecessors, with a partially hydraulic wing-folding mechanism, an analogue computer to set the torpedo's course, and a modern radio fit. It suffered a troubled development and a number were lost in unexplained crashes until the causes were identified and mitigated. The Barracuda finally entered squadron service in early 1943, and it was ready for operational use in July. The aircraft would not, however, see much combat until 1944.

TORPEDOES

The first British air-dropped torpedo in widespread use was the Mk VIII of 1914, with a warhead of 250lb or 500lb. This was the main torpedo used by the Fleet Air Arm in the interwar period. A development with a streamlined body, the Mk X was introduced in 1922, but production of this model ceased in 1929.

Various issues with air-dropped torpedoes were encountered between the wars, especially as aircraft speed rose. One difficulty experienced by the Fleet Air Arm was torpedoes becoming unstable as they were released due to interaction with the slipstream of the aircraft. One solution was Drum Control Gear (DCG) – a reel wound with weighted wire connecting the torpedo to the aircraft as it fell and keeping it steady. This was still in use in World War II. It worked, but prevented the torpedo-bomber from making an immediate turn away.

The Mk XI of 1934 pioneered 'burner cycle' propulsion in British use. It had the advantage over the previously favoured wet heater cycle (steam) power that no water was required and so there was no risk of freezing in flight. It had a warhead of 612lbs, and the ability to opt for higher speed and lower range (1,500 yards at 40 knots) or lower speed and higher range (4,000 yards at 27 knots). Various shortcomings were noted with the Mk XI. There were restrictions on speed and height of drop, problems with the torpedo rolling after release due to interaction with the aircraft's slipstream, and the afterbody was liable to break off if entry into the water was poor. An improved version in the form of the Mk XII was introduced shortly before the outbreak of war.

AXIS WARSHIPS

Many of the warships that the Fleet Air Arm's torpedo-bombers met in battle originated from the collapse of interwar naval treaties, and the arms race triggered by the Deutschland-class *panzerschiffe*. The latter vessels were an unconventional and brilliant response to the strictures of the Versailles Treaty. Germany was allowed to retain six obsolete pre-dreadnought battleships, and the terms permitted their replacement by modern ships when 20 years old. The new vessels were, however, restricted to 10,000 tons. It was expected that Germany would only be able to produce slow, short-range coastal defence ships at that tonnage.

Through technology and innovative design, the Deutschland-class warships proved to be well-suited to commerce raiding due to their long range (thanks to the fitment of eight economical diesel engines), relatively high speed (28.5 knots) and, most worryingly for the major naval powers, six 11in. main guns and eight 5.9in. secondary armament. The secondary armament alone matched most contemporary light cruisers.

The class set dominoes falling that would eventually lead to 40,000–50,000-ton battleships of 30+ knot performance. In the late 1920s, the French Marine Nationale

considered a small battlecruiser to counter Italian Trento-class fast cruisers. Instead, the Deutschland-class triggered the construction of the larger, more powerfully armed Dunkerque-class. These battlecruisers in turn prompted the German naval command to respond. The two ships of what became the Scharnhorst-class were originally to have been *panzerschiffe*, replacing the pre-dreadnoughts *Elsass*

The battleship *Scharnhorst* was built to a design that evolved from a battlecruiser, which emphasised speed and protection over endurance and reliability. This photograph shows the vessel's original bow, prior to it being modified to an 'Atlantic' profile with greater rake and flare. The low freeboard at the forward turrets could not be altered, however, leading to continual problems with weather damage. (Author's Collection)

and *Hessen*. A scheme for a 17,500 ton battlecruiser drawn in 1928 was updated to create a Dunkerque-beater, but Hitler was wary about provoking the major naval powers with ships that overtly exceeded treaty restrictions. Eventually he accepted vessels of 19,000 tons, but impressed upon the naval command to call them 'improved ships of 10,000 tons displacement' – eventual displacement was greater still.

The only element of the design remaining from the *panzerschiffe* was the main armament. New, larger calibre guns were not yet available, so the Scharnhorst-class would use nine of the same 28cm (11in.) guns, in modified Deutschland-class mountings, with the possibility that the ships could perhaps be 'upgunned' at some point in the future. The armour belt would be 350mm at its thickest, making the Scharnhorst-class somewhat 'over-armoured'. A large and potent powerplant was squeezed into tight machinery spaces, as the focus was on performance, with no intention for sustained operations in the open ocean. These compromises would result in frequent damage in bad weather, and much time spent on repairs.

The two hulls were laid down in September and October 1936, '*Ersatz Hessen*' at Deutsche Werke shipyard in Kiel and '*Ersatz Elass*' at Kriegsmarinewerft in Wilhelmshaven. At the time, Germany was still technically bound by the Versailles Treaty and other naval treaties, but the Anglo-German Naval Agreement of 1935, which imposed significantly relaxed restrictions on Germany, retrospectively legalised them. The first of the two ships (actually the second to be laid down) was launched on 3 October 1936 and named *Scharnhorst*. The other, named *Gneisenau*, followed in December, and they commissioned in January 1939 and May 1938, respectively.

The Anglo-German agreement paved the way for still larger ships, as long as the total tonnage of the Kriegsmarine did not exceed 35 per cent of that of the Royal Navy. Technically, any new battleships were not to exceed 35,000 tons, but the Second London Naval Treaty of March 1936 included a so-called 'escalator clause', which decreed that if any nation initiated a capital ship exceeding treaty limits, then the signatories may build battleships of up to 45,000 tons.

The German naval command was still focused on the Dunkerque-class when developing what would become the Bismarck-class. The shortcomings of the Scharnhorst-class were apparent even before the vessels had been commissioned, and the chief priority was to take advantage of a bigger displacement to create a better balanced design. The main armament was initially 330mm (13in.) guns (treaty limits were 16in.), and the main armour belt was to be 350mm (13.8in.) thick. However, when the naval command began to compare the design to planned foreign battleships, the main armament seemed inadequate.

German development of large-calibre guns had begun in secret as far back as 1934. With the Anglo-German agreement freeing Hitler from his fears of provoking the major naval powers, he pushed for a main armament of 380mm (15in.) guns. The increased weight led to a reduction in the main belt to compensate, although a greater proportion of the Bismarck-class's length would be covered by the main armour 'citadel' than most battleships.

A diesel powerplant like those of the *panzerschiffe* was considered, along with other innovative solutions such as turbo-electric propulsion, but a conventional oil-fired steam turbine powerplant was chosen, with similar layout to the Scharnhorst-class. The main dimensions were dictated by the size of existing docks and the depth of the Kiel Canal, but the resulting vessels would still be huge by any standards. The design was finalised on 1 July 1936, and the keel of the first ship (to be named *Bismarck*) was immediately laid down at Blohm & Voss, Hamburg, the second (*Tirpitz*) following at Kriegsmarinewerft in Wilhelmshaven in October.

The growing threat from aircraft was not ignored. From the end of World War I, anti-aircraft defences went from a few high-angle guns to a sophisticated integrated defensive system. Director-controlled artillery – guns laid by a central controller rather than individually – was commonplace by World War I, and was therefore a natural development for gunnery in three dimensions.

German designers aimed to solve the problems of naval anti-aircraft fire-control through extensive stabilisation. Both guns and directors were stabilised, which theoretically simplified the job of the fire-control systems by taking the ship's motion out of the equation and allowing the fire-control to concentrate on the movement of the attacking aircraft. From the first interwar development of naval anti-aircraft systems in the late 1920s, the stabilisation expanded from two axes to three, and advanced considerably in reliability and weight, although the final pre-war director for battleships still weighed 36,000kg.

Italy instituted a two-stage approach to compete with the Dunkerque-class – a relatively competitive modernisation first, with a significantly more capable new ship following some years later. Like France, Italy focused more on cruisers in the late 1920s and early 1930s, with vessels like the very fast Trento-class heavy cruiser being its primary weapon against the Marine Nationale. The Dunkerque-class shifted its focus to larger ships.

In November 1932, the Regia Marina's Admirals' Committee met to discuss proposals for new battleships capable of prevailing against the Dunkerque-class. Appended to the new proposals

Conte di Cavour was the first of four older dreadnought battleships modernised by the Regia Marina in the mid- to late-1930s. The modernisations were extensive, and significantly altered the ship's profile – most notably in the bow, which was lengthened and given sharp rake, and amidships, where one turret was removed and two close-set funnels gave a more modern appearance. (Author's Collection)

CONTE DI CAVOUR

The modernised battleship *Conte di Cavour* as it appeared on the night of 11 November 1940 when torpedoed at anchor at Taranto by Swordfish from *Illustrious*. Note the mix of secondary armament and heavy calibre anti-aircraft weapons, which illustrates the attempt made by the Regia Marina to find the best compromise with older weapons before new designs were available. *Conte di Cavour* suffered a single torpedo hit on the underside of the hull and was almost lost, sinking onto a sandbank up to its upperworks. The vessel's sister ship *Giulio Cesare* was similar, with only detail differences.

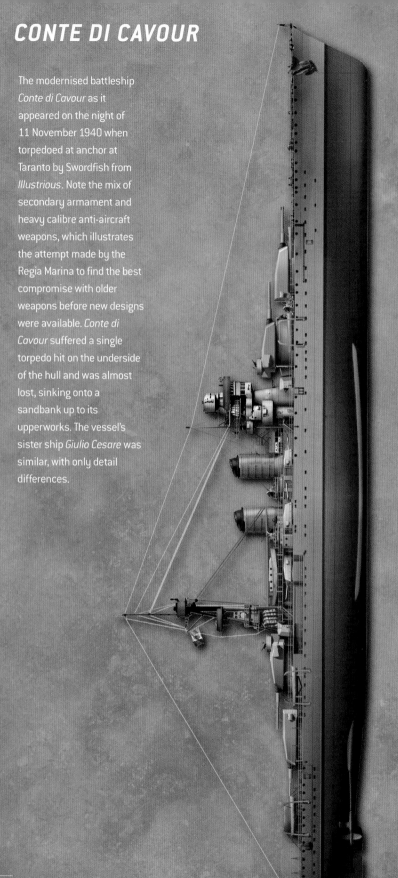

was a preliminary scheme to modernise the Regia Marina's World War I-era dreadnoughts of the Conte di Cavour- and Duilio-classes. These vessels were obsolete, but their hull form remained good by modern standards. Indeed, the medium-displacement new-build studies considered by the admirals used Conte di Cavour-class lines, and this indicated how the existing battleships might be rebuilt. Underwater protection had been a stumbling block for earlier modernisation studies, as naval architects did not think that an adequate level of defence could be addressed within the existing hull. The new-build proposals changed the thinking on this, and it was now thought feasible.

An unconventional approach was taken to armament. To free up weight for machinery of greatly increased power, one of the five 305mm (12in.) twin turrets would be removed, and the remaining guns improved by re-boring the barrels to 320mm. The increase in calibre, with a greater propellant charge, could make the guns as powerful as the 330mm weapons of the Dunkerque-class.

The modernisations demonstrated significant resource and manpower savings over new-builds, and, importantly, were permitted within the existing naval treaties. In October 1934, reconstruction of the two Conte di Cavour-class ships began at the CRDA shipyard in Trieste, and two new ships were laid down at Ansaldo, in Genoa, and at CRDA. These were the comprehensive solution to the Dunkerque-class problem – two battleships ostensibly on the 35,000-ton treaty maximum.

The desire for a balanced design with good general characteristics, as well as the speed and power to counter the Dunkerques, led to the size and displacement of the new design creeping up, despite the restrictions of the First London Naval Treaty of April 1930. By the time the design was finalised in 1934, patience with the treaties was running out. Italy and Japan declined to sign the Second London Naval Treaty in 1936, effectively ending restrictions on warship building, although the treaty nominally remained in force for the signatories until 1939. What emerged as the Littorio-class would be 40,000-ton, 735ft-long battleships armed with nine 15in. (381mm) guns and capable of speeds up to 30 knots. The design and fit-out of the Littorio-class in turn influenced the second pair of modernisations, the Duilio-class, initiated in 1937, which took advantage of the modern secondary and anti-aircraft weapons now available.

Key to the designs of both the rebuilt and new battleships was a novel system of underwater protection, conceived by Tenente Colonnello Umberto Pugliese, which promised excellent resistance to torpedoes and shells striking below the waterline. Experiments conducted on smaller ships created such confidence that all the rebuilt and newly constructed battleships would be equipped with it.

In response to the increasing threat from aircraft, whether carrier- or land-based, a sophisticated stabilised fire-control system was developed in the mid-1930s. However, the process of introducing modern guns took place somewhat later, with the result that up-to-date weapons were not widely available at the outbreak of war. This in turn meant that anti-aircraft batteries suffered from a lack of standardisation, with weapons of differing type, age and effectiveness fulfilling the same role across different ships and, in a few cases, on the same ship.

TECHNICAL SPECIFICATIONS

FLEET AIR ARM TORPEDO-BOMBERS

This Blackburn-built Swordfish of 835 NAS, being wheeled aft on the flightdeck of the escort carrier HMS *Battler* in May 1943, is armed with a practice torpedo for a training sortie. The Swordfish had recently been withdrawn from the frontline torpedo strike role. ASV aerials on the interplane struts have been blanked out by the censor. (Author's Collection)

The Fleet Air Arm operated four frontline torpedo-bomber designs during World War II, two of them biplanes and one of US origin – the Swordfish, Albacore, Barracuda and the Grumman Tarpon/Avenger. Only the first two had extensive use in the fleet torpedo-bomber role, while the Barracuda never attacked an Axis vessel more significant than a Flak ship with torpedoes, and the Tarpon never completed a torpedo strike in British service. According to Fleet Air Arm doctrine that combined torpedo-bomber and reconnaissance roles into the same aircraft, the crew of three consisted of a pilot, an Observer for navigation and a Telegraphist Air Gunner (TAG) to operate defensive armament and radio equipment.

The standard attack profile adopted by the Fleet Air Arm was to approach the target at medium altitude, out of effective range of anti-aircraft fire, before carrying out a steep dive to low-level just before launching the torpedo. Because of this requirement, Fleet Air Arm torpedo-bombers were effectively stressed for dive-bombing. The biplanes

needed no special adaptations, but the Barracuda relied on a novel design of flap that could act as a conventional high-lift device for take-off and landing, or create drag without lift in the dive.

The Swordfish was a conventional mid-1930s biplane of fabric-covered all-metal structure. The fuselage was based around a steel tube spaceframe, riveted up with fishplates and steel-sparred, light alloy-rib mainplanes, all of which were fabric-skinned apart from light alloy cowling panels at the nose. It was powered by a nine-cylinder Bristol Pegasus IIIM.3 radial engine of 630hp (or a 750hp Pegasus 30 in later variants), which gave a maximum speed of 138mph at 4,750ft. It was relatively large for a single-engined aircraft of low power, but a low wing-loading and high strength (the airframe was stressed to 9g) gave it impressive agility. As well as a single 18in. torpedo, the Swordfish could carry a variety of bombs and other stores on underwing carriers. Gun armament consisted of a single forward-facing Vickers 0.303in. machine gun, and a Lewis or Vickers K gun of the same calibre on a flexible Fairey pillar in the rear cockpit.

The Albacore was of more modern construction, with a fuselage skinned in light alloy (the forward part of steel-tube structure, the rear section stressed-skin) and a fully enclosed cockpit for all crew. The wings were still fabric-covered, but included hydraulic plain flaps on the lower mainplane. Other minor refinements included faired main undercarriage units and a cantilever tailplane. The engine was a newer, 1,130hp sleeve-valve Bristol Taurus VI radial, which was, however, considered less reliable than the Pegasus of the Swordfish. Its top speed was 159mph, some 20mph faster than the earlier machine, and it was more comfortable for the crew (which

A Mk XII torpedo being fitted to the Swordfish's interim replacement, the Albacore. The fabric-covering of the aircraft's wings is apparent, as are the semi-recessed bomb carriers, reducing drag somewhat, the aluminium-clad fuselage and streamlined undercarriage units. (Author's Collection)

As the Albacore was designed with fully enclosed crew positions, unlike the Swordfish, it required an opening aft section to allow the defensive gun to be used. The hinged clamshell, forming a windshield for the gunner when open, was similar to the arrangement on the Battle light bomber. The rear 0.303in. Vickers K gun (here lacking an ammunition drum) was mounted on a Fairey pillar, and some boasted a reflector sight, as here. (Author's Collection)

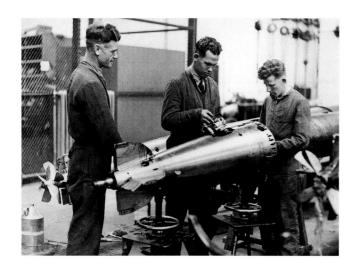

helped them maintain efficiency in poor conditions for longer), although it was less manoeuvrable.

The Barracuda was an all-metal monoplane with a shoulder-mounted wing. The forward fuselage was a heavily engineered steel tube structure, while the wings and rear fuselage were stressed-skinned. Power was from a Rolls-Royce Merlin 32 offering 1,640hp at 2,000ft, which gave the Barracuda a top speed of 228mph. It incorporated an innovative Fairey-Youngman flap, that could be used as a conventional landing and take-off aid, an auxiliary aerofoil to increase cruising efficiency and a dive brake (by tilting the trailing edge upwards instead of down). The torpedo used was the same Mk XII* employed by the Swordfish and Albacore, but the Barracuda included a Type F torpedo director – an analogue computer interpreting crew inputs to set the torpedo gyros for more precise targeting than the rudimentary sights of the biplanes.

Technicians work on a Mk XII torpedo just before World War II. The afterbody they are assembling contains the motor and gyros, one of which the middle technician is holding, for propulsion and control. The eight-bladed contra-rotating propeller can be seen on the torpedo behind. The middle section of the torpedo was the air vessel, containing compressed air, while the explosive warhead was installed in the fore part. (Author's Collection)

Defensive armament was a Vickers 0.303in. gun on a flexible mount in the rear cockpit, later changed to a twin gun. The Observer could also operate a Vickers K gun firing out of the side windows, which were removable for that purpose, but it was a complicated arrangement and the gun was rarely if ever carried.

The Tarpon/Avenger was a modern three-seat torpedo and level/glide bomber of stressed-skin construction, featuring a power-operated rear turret. It was powered by a 1,600hp Wright R-2600 radial engine and had a top speed of 271mph. The aircraft was built to US specifications and did not meet Fleet Air Arm requirements for a torpedo-bomber, being acquired mainly for the anti-submarine role. It could not carry the British 18in. torpedo, and the Fleet Air Arm only obtained a small number of the appropriate 22.4in. torpedo.

Mk XII TORPEDO

The Mk XII and its improved Mk XII* derivative were the Fleet Air Arm's standard torpedoes between 1937 and 1945. They were steel-bodied, 16ft 2in. long and weighed 1,620–1,660lbs depending on the type of explosive in the warhead. The Mk XII* had gyro angling, allowing a specific course to be set before launch. Initially, speed of drop was restricted to 150 knots (173mph), which was not a particular problem for the sluggish Swordfish and Albacores, but with the advent of the faster Barracuda, improvements were made to the tail and propellers to allow the Mk XII* to be released at a greater velocity. The torpedo ran off atomised paraffin driving a four-cylinder radial engine, which gave the weapon a maximum speed of 40 knots.

TORPEDOES

The standard air-dropped torpedo in use by the Fleet Air Arm in 1939 was the 18in. Mk XII. The improved Mk XII* model later became the standard weapon across both the RAF and the Fleet Air Arm.

A significant development from 1938 was a firing pistol triggered by a Duplex Coil Rod (DCR), allowing the torpedo to be detonated by magnetic influence, as well as or instead of direct contact, depending on how the torpedo was set. With the 'duplex pistol', the torpedo could be set to run underneath the hull of an enemy warship and explode beneath the keel at a point where there was relatively little protection, and an explosion would do most

The analogue 'computor' that was the 'brains' of the Type F Torpedo Director fire control system fitted in the Barracuda. The two main controls can be seen at the top – the wind speed dial in the middle and, at top right, a dial to set wind direction and the direction of the target ship. This could be continually altered during the run-in to take account of evasive manoeuvres by the vessel being targeted, setting the gyros in the torpedo to assume the correct course. (Author's Collection)

harm to the ship's structure. The disadvantage was a relatively narrow window of proximity to the hull in which the DCR would work, so torpedo settings relied heavily on judgement. In rough water it became hard to assess the appropriate depth to set, and it could be sensitive to external conditions, sometimes exploding prematurely or not at all.

The DCR working as advertised was a significant factor in the success at Taranto, but its shortcomings were highlighted against *Bismarck*. From 1943, the DCR was phased out, and the only alternative for the Fleet Air Arm for the duration of the war was the old Mk IIA contact pistol. A further improved torpedo, the Mk XV, with longer range and greater strength, was available from 1942, and it was the main weapon used by the Barracuda.

British aerial torpedoes were somewhat slow, hence the preference of the Fleet Air Arm to attack from the bow so as to avoid a ship at speed being able to effectively outrun a torpedo until its maximum range was reached.

Maintaining the torpedo in a steady and controlled descent after release from the aircraft led to work on better solutions than DCG, and trials in the late 1930s assessed horizontal stabilising fins (known as Air Rudders) at various spans, with and without DCG. Air Rudders evolved into the Monoplane Air Tail Mk IV, which was a large 'wing' with prominent end plates that was gyroscope-controlled and angled to keep the torpedo at the ideal attitude as it fell, finally obviating the need for the DCG.

The method of aiming the torpedo on the Swordfish and Albacore was basic. A row of lights was arranged on either side of the cockpit ahead of the pilot that allowed him to judge the correct 'lay-off' – in other words, the amount they had to aim the aircraft ahead of the target in order that the torpedo struck where intended. This required the pilot to fly at a specific speed and altitude, and accurately judge the speed and distance of the target ship. Each light was spaced to represent an additional five knots of target ship speed.

This was adequate for aircraft of the performance of the Swordfish and Albacore, and it relied on the judgement and precision of the pilot, so accuracy could suffer when he was less trained or experienced. A more reliable solution for higher performance aircraft was the Type F Torpedo Director. This consisted of an analogue computer taking inputs from the pilot or Observer that adjusted the torpedo's course-setting gyros during the run-in. Thus, the pilot aimed the aircraft directly at the target ship and could adjust for its course and estimated speed during the run in.

AXIS WARSHIPS

The Scharnhorst-class reflected the straitened circumstances of its birth – a 32,000-ton ship with excellent performance and good armour protection but relatively weak armament and poor reliability. After initial trials, *Gneisenau* demonstrated that the slim bow and low freeboard allowed even moderate seas to inundate the forward parts of the ship, rendering A-turret unusable. Both vessels were soon rebuilt with an 'Atlantic bow' of greater length, height, flare and rake. Even so, the Scharnhorst-class still suffered flooding and water damage to systems throughout their short lives.

The main armament was nine 28cm (11in.) guns, in triple mountings. The main armour belt was 350mm at its thickest. Protection against an underwater explosion, such as by an air-dropped torpedo, consisted of a conventional multi-layer system, with a series of bulkheads and void spaces designed to disperse and redirect the energy from a detonation. Torpedo protection was strong amidships but weakened significantly towards the ends. Parsons geared turbines from Brown, Boveri & Cie of Switzerland delivered 160,000hp via three shafts, allowing an impressive 32 knots.

The Bismarck-class ships were considerably larger than the Scharnhorst-class, at 52,000 tons fully load, but designed along similar lines and layout. The main armour belt of the Bismarck-class was actually thinner at its point of maximum thickness than that of the Scharnhorst-class, but in all other respects, armour protection was more extensive. Underwater protection echoed the Scharnhorst-class, with the same strengths and flaws. Unlike the earlier battleships, the Bismarck-class had excellent seakeeping, although the broad beam and low metacentric height introduced to reduce instability from flooding resulted in a short roll period. This made them uncomfortable in a sea and less than ideal gun platforms, particularly for anti-aircraft fire.

The ship was driven by a three-shaft powerplant comprising high, medium and low pressure Curtis geared turbines driving a single reduction gear, each shaft producing a nominal 46,000hp. When 'forced' this could produce as much as 150,170hp for a speed of just over 30 knots.

The Admiral Hipper-class cruisers were often partners to the larger ships in commerce-raiding operations. Like the

The port-midships heavy anti-aircraft battery and port aft director tower of *Scharnhorst* or *Gneisenau*, photographed early in the war. (Author's Collection)

Deutschland-class, they were designed as powerful surface raiders, and were considerably larger and somewhat better protected than most 'treaty cruisers'. The decision to power them with high-pressure steam turbines in contrast to the Deutschland-class's diesels made them short-legged and unreliable, however. They were armed with eight 20.3cm (8in.) guns, with a secondary armament of 10.5cm (4.1in.) dual-purpose guns typically used in the anti-aircraft role, but which could be used against surface combatants.

The Regia Marina favoured high performance in its battleships and cruisers, but, particularly once the restrictions of the London and Washington naval treaties had been shrugged off, succeeded in producing well-balanced designs without major compromises. One advantage enjoyed by Italy was that service in the Mediterranean did not require long range, so ships did not have to carry as much fuel as some competitors, and accommodation for the crew could be more restricted.

Unusually among European navies, Italy decided to respond to new capital ships from its competitors with both new-build ships and extensive modernisations of older vessels. The rebuilds gutted the existing dreadnoughts and created a substantially new ship within the hull. The Conte di Cavour-class had a new-profile bow built around the old, leaving the original profile encased within a new structure. With the Duilio-class rebuilds, the old bow was dismantled when the new bow was added. New machinery almost tripled the available power, with Belluzzo geared turbines of 90,000hp in a two-shaft arrangement raising top speed from 21 knots to 26.

The original main armament consisted of 305mm (12in.) guns in two triple and three twin turrets. The midships twin turret, which had excessively restricted firing arcs, was removed, and the remaining guns modified to increase their bore (to 320mm) and propellant charge.

The new Littorio-class were able to address all of the shortcomings of the rebuilt battleships, with significantly greater size and displacement allowing all the Regia Marina's requirements to be met without compromise. They displaced 40,000 tons and were armed with nine 381mm (15in.) guns in three triple turrets. The powerplant was similar to that of the rebuilt battleships, but offered 128,000hp, which propelled the Littorio-class to 30 knots.

The Littorio-class armour scheme aimed to protect the ship against shells of the same calibre as its own main guns. This included a 280mm (11in.) thick main belt, surmounted by a 70mm (2.8in.) 'decapping plate' designed to remove the cap of an armour-piercing shell before it travelled deep into the hull.

Underwater protection was trusted to the aforementioned 'Pugliese System' – longitudinal cylinders located inside the turn of the bilge designed to absorb and disperse the energy from a detonation, preventing the shock being received by the structure of the hull. The cylinder was enclosed within a watertight bulkhead, and the space around the cylinder always kept filled with liquid. The cylinder was designed to collapse when subjected to a blow like an explosion, absorbing kinetic energy and ensuring the integrity of the inner bulkheads. What resulted would be controlled flooding, limited to certain non-vital areas of the hull, and incoming water was directed downwards and toward the centreline via 'automatic balancing channels'.

Like many underwater protection arrangements, the Pugliese system gave its best protection amidships, diminishing towards the ends. The cylinder tapered at either

Two of the four Zara-class cruisers, including the lead ship launched in 1931, are seen here sailing in the Mediterranean in November 1935. These vessels were fast, well-armed and well protected. They were capable of a range of 3,200 miles at a cruising speed of 25 knots, but given the restricted nature of the Mediterranean, were not required to spend long periods at sea, unlike their Royal Navy equivalents. (Author's Collection)

end and did not cover the bow and stern at all, the weight and volume of the cylinder balanced against the protection it offered for machinery spaces and magazines. It was best realised in the Littorio-class ships, which were designed with it in mind. The Conte di Cavour- and Duilio-class vessels were slightly more compromised in their execution, with smaller diameter cylinders of 114m in length and less void space.

The Italian cruisers that supported the battleships in a scouting and screening role had a similar focus on out-and-out performance, although there was later a tendency towards better balanced vessels. The first Italian heavy cruisers were the slender Trento-class of the mid-late 1920s, the first of which reached almost 36 knots in trials. They proved fragile once in service, with armour barely sufficient to stand up against a light cruiser. The succeeding Zara-class had significantly better armour protection, with a 150mm (6in.) main belt and 70mm (2.8in.) deck plating. Despite this additional weight, they were capable of a still-impressive 32 knots courtesy of a lightweight, two-shaft powerplant. Additionally, the Zaras had good seakeeping qualities, especially by Regia Marina standards. While technically 'treaty cruisers,' all four vessels exceeded the mandated displacement by some margin.

AXIS ANTI-AIRCRAFT WEAPONRY

Anti-aircraft artillery was one area in which the Kriegsmarine lagged behind other naval nations, thanks to the Treaty of Versailles prohibiting Germany from developing automatic guns. This was mitigated somewhat by German industry setting up subsidiaries overseas, allowing the development of weapons such as the Rhinemetall-Borsigg Flak 30 light anti-aircraft gun in Switzerland. The German-developed medium naval anti-aircraft gun, the 3.7cm SKC/30, on the other hand, was required to be a hand-loaded, single-shot weapon.

In other respects, though, such as stabilisation, Kriegsmarine anti-aircraft artillery was advanced, although it is unclear whether this improved the success of the system or merely increased its complication.

The Kriegsmarine settled on a three-tier system of defence against aircraft, with a heavy 10.5cm gun, a medium 3.7cm gun and a light 2cm autocannon. The heavy gun was controlled by the director, while the lighter guns were laid independently, albeit with the benefit of some information from the director. Unlike its rivals, the Kriegsmarine did not combine the anti-destroyer and heavy anti-aircraft armament of battleships and cruisers into a single dual-purpose gun.

The director plotted the observed position of the target aircraft at a number of points, drawing an average line through the latter to smooth out the data and feeding the information gathered into an analogue computer to predict the future position,

3.7cm SKC/30

The standard Kriegsmarine medium anti-aircraft gun between 1939 and 1943, the 3.7cm SKC/30 was a long-barrelled weapon with a bore length of 80 calibres, leading to a high muzzle velocity. Although it technically outranged the 40mm Bofors, its typical rate of fire of 30–40 rounds-per-minute was a fraction of the Swedish autocannon's, due to it being a hand-loaded, semi-automatic weapon. The SKC/30 was not director-controlled, but in 1943 a new sight provided target and wind speed from the director, and calculated deflections automatically. The SKC/30 was available in single and twin mountings (the latter depicted here), operated by a crew of six, with manual training and elevation only. It was, however, automatically stabilised.

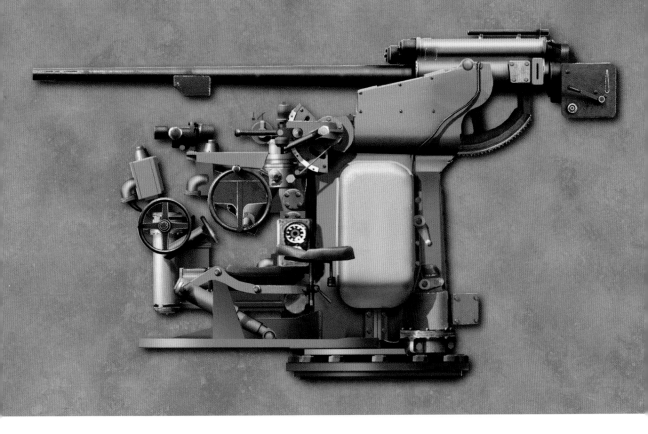

which would be used to orient the guns and set the range of the shells. Oscillations in pitch, roll and yaw were theoretically cancelled out by gyro-stabilised mounts on both the gun and the director. Kriegsmarine fire-control system computers therefore needed only to adjust for the course and speed of the aircraft, the forward speed of the ship and wind speed/direction – in theory, at least.

The Type 1933 Director was the first to adopt the distinctive spherical shield, known as 'Wackelkopf' (nodding head) or possibly 'Wackeltopf' (Chinese wok). It was employed in the battleships *Scharnhorst* and *Gneisenau* and the heavy cruisers *Admiral Hipper* and *Blücher*. A much-improved version, saving 8,000kg and with superior function and reliability, was introduced in 1937 on the Bismarck-class battleships and the cruiser *Prinz Eugen*. The director controlled stabilisation of the 10.5cm guns as well as their firing solution.

The 10.5cm/65 SKC/33 was the main heavy anti-aircraft gun used on Kriegsmarine cruisers and capital ships in World War II. Its large bore-length of 60 calibres (the '65' designation refers to the whole barrel) compares with the Royal

A twin mounting of the 3.7cm SKC/30 medium Flak gun, fitted to all major Kriegsmarine warships in the first part of the war, is fully manned for a live fire exercise. Note the Flak-Entfernungsmesser to the right operating a portable rangefinder. (Author's Collection)

A Kriegsmarine sailor poses with a quad-2cm/65 C/38 Flak installation, known as the 'Vierling' ('Quadruplet'). This gun was based on a design developed in Switzerland, allowing Germany to avoid a ban on the development of automatic weapons. (Author's Collection)

Navy 4.5in. QF gun of 45 calibres. The longer barrel meant the trunnions had to be close to the breech to avoid a high centre of gravity in the installation and still allow high elevation. This necessitated large counterweights on top of the breech.

The long barrel also conferred a high muzzle velocity – 2,952ft per second (900m per second) compared with 2,449ft per second (746m per second) for the 4.5in. QF. Rate of fire was a maximum of 18 rounds per minute, with an average rate of 15 rounds. At an elevation of 80 degrees, the gun's ceiling was 41,010ft (12,500m), but it became ineffective from roughly 10,000ft (3,000m) due to limitations in the mountings' training and elevation speed.

The initial mount for this gun was the twin Dopp LC/31 from the earlier 8.8cm Flak. Training was controlled by electrically driven hydraulics, while elevation and cross-levelling were driven by electric motors, and there was also electrically assisted loading. Improved versions were the LC/31d and LC/31gE, reflecting lessons from the Spanish Civil War, with significant differences such as a separate cradle for each barrel. The 1931 mounting and its derivatives were seen on Deutschland-, Scharnhorst- and Hipper-class ships. Remote power control (RPC) was available in cross-levelling and partially in elevation.

In 1937, the twin LC/37 mount was introduced, with further improvements and simplifications, including a return to a single cradle and full RPC. *Bismarck* had four LC/31 mounts forward and four LC/37s aft for its entire career, while *Tirpitz* only received the full complement of LC/37s in late 1941 when the two aftermost mountings were replaced. The Scharnhorst-class battleships received this mounting while in Brest in 1941–42 prior to the 'Channel Dash'. The mounting was open at the rear, and its lack of waterproofing led to problems with the electrics in rough weather, especially on the wetter ships.

The weakest link within the Kriegsmarine's anti-aircraft systems for most of the war was the medium gun, the 3.7cm (1.45in.) SKC/30. Despite its shortcomings, this weapon was installed in the majority of Kriegsmarine surface warships.

The medium and light anti-aircraft guns were not director controlled, but in 1943 a sophisticated sight for the SKC/30 was introduced in which target and wind data were supplied directly to the sight from the director, and deflections calculated in the sight itself. By this time, however, the gun was being replaced by the fully automatic 40mm Bofors.

The 3.7cm gun was another comparatively long-barrelled weapon, with a bore length of 80 calibres leading to a fast muzzle velocity of 3,281ft per second (1,000m per second), compared with 2,801ft per second (854m per second) for the Bofors. The 3.7cm SKC/30 had an effective ceiling of 22,310ft (6,800m), which was actually some 2,000ft (610m) higher than the Bofors, but in terms of rate of fire, the two guns were worlds apart. The Bofors could put up to 120 rounds in the air per minute, per barrel, with a typical rate of 80–90 rounds. The 3.7cm SKC/30 had a maximum rate of fire of 80 rounds per gun per minute, but a typical rate of 30–40.

The SKC/30 was available in single and twin versions, although the latter was most common by the outbreak of war. The twin mounting was a tri-axially stabilised twin Dopp LC/30 – essentially a scaled-down version of the mounting developed for the 8.8cm gun and later adapted for the 10.5cm. This was operated by a crew of six, with manual training and elevation only.

Light anti-aircraft weaponry on Kriegsmarine warships took the form of the ubiquitous 2cm/65 C/30 or C/38 weapon. Unlike the 3.7cm gun, this was a modern, automatic weapon which, in its C/38 model at least, was effective and reliable. It was based on the ST-5 cannon developed by Swiss company Solothurn (a subsidiary of Rheinmetall) in the 1920s. Rheinmetall duly took over development of the gun in Germany for the Kriegsmarine.

The earlier C/30 model had a small, 20-round magazine, necessitating frequent changes, and was prone to jamming. It had an effective rate of fire of 120 rounds per minute. The C/38 had a magazine twice the capacity of the earlier gun and better performance and reliability, with a rate of fire of 220 rounds per minute. It was available in single, twin and, from 1940, the familiar quad 'Vierling' mounting. The numbers of these guns on Kriegsmarine warships tended to increase significantly over their lifespan. *Scharnhorst* was originally fitted with ten C/30 guns in single mounts, and by the time of its sinking in December 1943 the warship had 22 – ten in single and 12 in quadruple mounts.

Bismarck survivors indicated that control of the short-range weapons was independent of the 10.5cm guns, and at ranges below 1,000m the vessel effectively relied on its 3.7cm and 20mm guns.

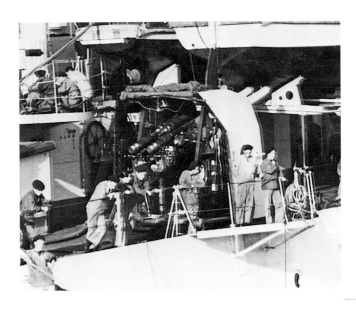

This 100mm/47 OTO Mod 1928 heavy anti-aircraft gun was fitted to the Italian Trento-class heavy cruiser *Trieste*. The weapon's close-set barrels allowed both to be mounted on the same cradle, saving weight, but leading to significant shell interference in flight, reducing accuracy. (NHHC image NH 111451)

The Regia Marina's anti-aircraft director was based on Barr & Stroud's 'flyplane' concept which reduced a complex problem to a small number of constant factors, such as the speed of the target aircraft, and a single variable – the changing angle of the target relative to the gunner. The system made it theoretically possible to quickly calculate a firing solution and check its accuracy while firing to feed back into

This photograph of the battleship *Italia*, formerly *Littorio*, taken shortly after the war, reveals a concentration of anti-aircraft weapons amidships. Six port 90mm/50 Ansaldo Mod 1938-9 guns in individual streamlined mountings can be seen atop raised pedestals (protecting stabilisation mechanisms from heavy seas) on the main deck, while a row of 37mm cannon sit above them on the shelter deck. To the right of the latter weapons is the port anti-aircraft gun director tower. (Author's Collection)

the system. In reality, the method of calculating the predicted course of the target took a few seconds, which could be a long time during an engagement.

The Regia Marina, like the Kriegsmarine, did not develop a fully dual-purpose gun for the secondary battery on battleships and cruisers. This avoided certain compromises in the weapon, but complicated ammunition storage and supply, and added weight.

A new 90mm heavy anti-aircraft gun was developed during the late 1930s, but it was not ready when the modernisations of *Conte di Cavour* and *Giulio Cesare* were due for completion. These battleships were therefore armed with the 120mm 120/50 OTO Model 1933 gun in three twin turrets on either side, and the 100mm 100/47 OTO Mod 1928 gun in two twin turrets per side.

The 120/50 was based on a 1926-vintage destroyer main armament – a traditional weapon with separate projectile and propellant, with a maximum rate of fire of just seven rounds per minute. The gun also suffered from high dispersion of salvos. Its maximum ceiling was just over 35,000ft, and it could not elevate above 42 degrees. The 100/47 was more modern, with fixed ammunition and a better rate of fire of eight to ten rounds per minute. This gun, based on a pre-World War I Austro-Hungarian weapon, was regarded as a good anti-aircraft weapon by the Regia Marina. Four twin mounts elevating up to 85 degrees were installed on the rebuilt Conte di Cavours. This was also the main heavy anti-aircraft gun on Regia Marina cruisers, with six to eight such mountings installed on light cruisers and eight on heavy cruisers.

The Duilio-class rebuilds and the new Littorio-class used the 1939-pattern 90mm 90/50 Ansaldo gun, which represented a significant advance on the weapons employed by the Conte di Cavours. This had fixed ammunition and a rate of fire of 12 rounds per minute, with an anti-aircraft ceiling of 35,000ft (10,800m). They were installed in a new specially developed streamlined turret, shaped to mitigate overpressure from the main guns, each mounting only a single gun. The mountings were quad-axially stabilised, leading to considerable complexity within the mechanisms.

Operationally, the gun was only fitted on the Duilio- and Littorio-class battleships, the former mounting five on each beam on the shelter deck, while the latter had an additional pair. The guns on the Duilio-class ships had their stabilisation removed

BREDA 37mm/54

The Breda 37mm/54 calibre water-cooled, gas-operated autocannon was the Regia Marina's standard medium anti-aircraft gun. It had a maximum rate of fire of 120 rounds per minute and an effective range of 5,000ft (1,500m). The 37mm/54 was initially available in single and twin stabilised mountings, and later both an air-cooled twin mounting and a 'disappearing' single mounting were produced. Training and elevation (up to 80 degrees on the twin mounts and 90 degrees on the single) was manual. It was an effective weapon, but it suffered from excessive vibration. The crew was made up of a gun captain, layer, trainer, two loaders and two ammunition handlers.

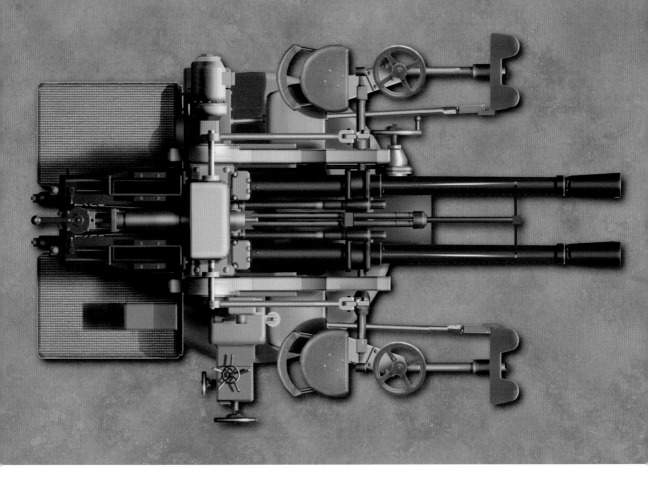

following the disastrous Operation *K7* in February 1942, when flooding ruined the electrics on *Duilio*'s starboard battery, rendering it useless until the ship could return to port. The stabilisation mechanisms for the battery were disembarked, partly to improve the guns' poor-weather reliability and partly to help reduce topweight. The 90mm battery on the Littorio-class ships was less susceptible to high seas, so the newer ships retained their stabilisation.

In the early interwar period, the Regia Marina used the British two-pounder pom-pom gun as its medium anti-aircraft weapon, but from 1930 it sought an up-to-date replacement. The result was the Breda 37mm/54 calibre, a water-cooled, gas-operated autocannon. Different rates of fire could be selected – 60, 90 or 120 rounds per minute maximum. While the magazines contained only six rounds, they could be fed into the gun's 'hopper' in sequence, which helped maintain a rapid rate of fire. It was initially available in single and twin mountings, which had basic stabilisation. In 1938,

A twin Breda 37mm/54 medium anti-aircraft gun on board the battleship *Duilio*. This weapon was a modern autocannon with good performance, but it suffered from vibration due to its gas-operated mechanism transmitting significant recoil to the hull. (Author's Collection)

a simpler air-cooled twin mount was introduced, and in 1939, a 'disappearing' single mount for installation on the foredeck of the Duilios and Littorios. All mountings were manually trained and elevated. Effective range was 5,000ft (1,500m). Twelve guns were fitted on the Conte di Cavours, 15 on the Duilios and 20 on the Littorios (with further guns added as the war progressed). The gun was well-respected in Regia Marina service, and it appears to have been effective at defending against low-flying aircraft. However, the twin mountings suffered from vibration due to the rigid mounts necessary for the gas-operated mechanism. This tended to reduce accuracy during sustained firing, and limited installation to parts of the ship with sufficiently strong structure to withstand the vibration.

At the outbreak of war, the 1931-pattern 13.2mm Breda machine gun was the primary short-range defence weapon, but the 20mm/65 Breda M1935 (enlarged from the 13.2mm gun) was under development. As with the 37mm, the 20mm was available in single and twin mounts, the latter demonstrating a unique configuration with the left hand gun set diagonally above the right. It was air-cooled and gas-operated. By 1940, the 20mm/65 was replacing 13.2mm guns throughout major Regia Marina warships.

In this stern view of *Italia*, the two twin 20mm/65 Breda M1935 gun mounts sited on the aft main turret (housing three 381mm guns) are clearly visible. (Author's Collection)

THE STRATEGIC SITUATION

In September 1939, the Royal Navy faced the threat of Kriegsmarine warships harrying Britain's supply lines. The three *panzerschiffe* were well established in service and two were at sea in their planned area of operation when war was declared. *Gneisenau* had just returned to service following modifications to improve its seaworthiness and *Scharnhorst* would join the vessel in November when its own modifications were complete. The two Bismarck-class battleships were fitting out, having been launched the previous year, but they were some way from operational status. The Kriegsmarine would not be able to countenance a full-scale battle with a numerically superior Royal Navy, so its strategic focus was on commerce raiding, only engaging its enemy should local superiority be gained.

The Royal Navy, therefore, had little expectation of facing a fleet action, and questions were raised about the utility of the Fleet Air Arm. Winston Churchill, First Lord of the Admiralty, complained in January 1940 that 'There are very few surface ships of the enemy, and one can only consider the possible break-out of a German raider or fast battleship as potential targets. Provision must be made for this; but certainly it does not justify anything like this immense expenditure'. Churchill proposed that the Fleet Air Arm take responsibility for coastal defence from the RAF, further weakening its already thin resources at sea.

In fact, the break-out of *Deutschland* and *Graf Spee* required considerable effort from the Fleet Air Arm – most of the Royal Navy's carriers joined the hunt for the raiders. The Fleet Air Arm was heavily engaged in Norway from April 1940, but there was little to do in the torpedo-bomber role. Opportunities were few, and those that

arose were wasted. Lord Beaverbrook, Minister for Aircraft Production, put development of new naval aircraft on hold in May 1940 and diverted resources away from naval aircraft production. To the casual observer, the Fleet Air Arm, and its torpedo force in particular, seemed peripheral to the Allied war effort.

This changed dramatically in June 1940 when Norway fell and France surrendered. Britain had lost a major ally and a significant counter to the Kriegsmarine's capital ships. German vessels could now operate from Norway into the Atlantic, as *Admiral Scheer* successfully did in December 1940, and even from French ports. This fear became a reality when, after Operation *Berlin* in January–March 1941, *Scharnhorst* and *Gneisenau* put into Brest.

The head of the Kriegsmarine, Großadmiral Erich Raeder, boards a new warship for an inspection shortly before the war. Raeder, more than any other individual, shaped the form that the Kriegsmarine took in 1939. Due to his ambitions to build a conventional battle fleet, the Kriegsmarine possessed some extremely powerful capital ships, but it was structured imperfectly for both cruiser warfare and traditional fleet engagements. (Author's Collection)

The German surface warship programme in the 1930s was incoherent, starting out as a plan for 'Kreuzerkrieg' (cruiser warfare) but evolving in an ad hoc manner into a battle fleet that could meet the Royal Navy on equal terms by the mid-1940s. The head of the Kriegsmarine, Großadmiral Erich Raeder, had been reassured by Hitler that war with the naval powers could be avoided in 1939. When this proved incorrect, the Kriegsmarine went to war with a force that met requirements for neither strategy.

This hampered the Kriegsmarine's commerce-raiding ability, but the few conventional capital ships completed by the end of 1940 were powerful enough to overwhelm Royal Navy cruisers and even defeat most of their capital ships on an individual basis. This meant convoys needed heavy escorts. It was apparent by early 1941 that warships acting as raiders could not destroy as much Allied shipping as U-boats or even auxiliary cruisers, but they had a particular value in disrupting Allied activity and forcing a resource-heavy response.

The Oberkommando der Kriegsmarine wrote in a tactical note in May 1941 that 'The first battleship operation [Operation *Berlin*], as well as the operations of the cruiser *Hipper*, have demonstrated, in addition to the considerable tactical successes, the substantial strategic effects that can be achieved by such a deployment of surface forces. These strategic effects extend not only to the sea area chosen as the theatre of operations, but also spill over into other theatres of war'. The author of the note added that with Britain's 'Protection of his convoys he has evidently approached the limit of what is possible for him, and that he can make his decisive reinforcements of security only if he weakens positions important to him (Mediterranean, homeland), or restricts convoy traffic'.

In addition to the increased threat posed to Britain by the Kriegsmarine, from June 1940 the nation was at war in a new theatre, the Mediterranean. Here, sea power was paramount, and the chances of meeting a modern battle fleet in action were very real. The loss of the French Navy as an ally in the western Mediterranean meant that the

One of the 22 merchant ships sunk by *Scharnhorst* and *Gneisenau*, seen from the latter being subjected to gunfire and burning, during the raider cruise Operation *Berlin* in January–March 1941. (Author's Collection)

Royal Navy had to introduce forces in that region to compensate. Force H was based at Gibraltar and was built around the carrier *Ark Royal* and a small number of capital ships. Meanwhile, the Mediterranean Fleet was bolstered with additional battleships and the modern carrier HMS *Illustrious*. This in turn weakened the Home Fleet and limited the Royal Navy's ability to act in other theatres.

The Regia Marina possessed considerable local strength, and the benefit that it would not face demands from other theatres that would weaken it. While Italy considered France its principal adversary, from the 1920s the Regia Marina eyed the Royal Navy warily. Il Duce, Benito Mussolini, complained that he was 'imprisoned' by the Royal Navy, whose naval bases at Alexandria, in Egypt, Malta and Gibraltar allowed it to control the entry routes to the Mediterranean and police the sea lanes between Italy and North Africa.

When Italy declared war, the Royal Navy was relatively weak in the Mediterranean, and the fleet was reinforced significantly in the latter half of 1940. There were no operational Fleet Air Arm squadrons available to carry out attacks at first, so a training unit of Swordfish, 767 NAS, was hastily made operational and sent to bomb Genoa. By October, the modern carriers *Ark Royal* and *Illustrious* were in theatre, supplementing the old HMS *Eagle*.

Italy's strategic power was bound up in its navy. Here, a Regia Marina taskforce led by the battleship *Conte di Cavour* crosses the Adriatic in late 1939 to back up Italy's demands that Albania submit to 'protective occupation'. (Author's Collection)

For Italy, the usefulness of aircraft carriers quickly became apparent, and construction of two was initiated, but lack of resources meant these progressed slowly and neither was ready before Italy surrendered in 1943. The Royal Navy's torpedo-bomber force gave it a reach with ship-killing weapons that was not open to Italy, forcing the Regia Marina to try to develop alternatives, such as Maiale 'human torpedoes' and MT explosive motorboats.

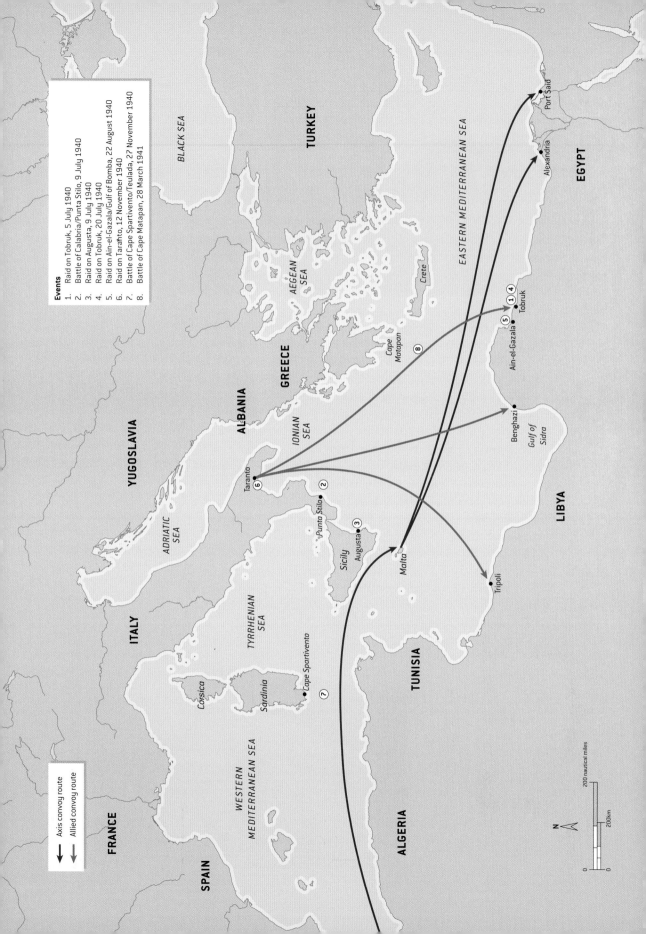

Events

1. Raid on Tobruk, 5 July 1940
2. Battle of Calabria/Punta Stilo, 9 July 1940
3. Raid on Augusta, 9 July 1940
4. Raid on Tobruk, 20 July 1940
5. Raid on Ain-el-Gazala/Gulf of Bomba, 22 August 1940
6. Raid on Taranto, 12 November 1940
7. Battle of Cape Spartivento/Teulada, 27 November 1940
8. Battle of Cape Matapan, 28 March 1941

Axis convoy route

Allied convoy route

BLACK SEA

TURKEY

EGYPT

Port Said

Alexandria

EASTERN MEDITERRANEAN SEA

Tobruk ① ④

Ain-el-Gazala ⑤

Benghazi

Gulf of Sidra

LIBYA

Tripoli

AEGEAN SEA

Crete

Cape Matapan

⑧

GREECE

ALBANIA

IONIAN SEA

Taranto ⑥

Punta Stilo

②

Augusta ③

Sicily

Malta

YUGOSLAVIA

ADRIATIC SEA

ITALY

TYRRHENIAN SEA

Corsica

Sardinia

Cape Spartivento ⑦

TUNISIA

ALGERIA

WESTERN MEDITERRANEAN SEA

FRANCE

SPAIN

N

200 nautical miles

200km

Following Italy's invasion of Abyssinia in 1935, the Royal Navy's strategic focus shifted from a likely war to trade protection in the east. Italian control of the sea threatened Allied interests in North Africa and the Middle East, particularly the Suez Canal and access to oil from Saudi Arabia and Iran, and the British colony of Malta, just over 50 miles from Sicily. The Egyptian government was wary of Italy after the annexation of Abyssinia, and permitted the large-scale presence of British military forces within its borders. This was uncomfortably close to Italy's colony in Libya, and threatened to separate Italy from its East African colonies too.

Malta represented both a strength and a weakness to the Royal Navy. It was ideally placed as a base to strike at shipping between Italy and North Africa, but its proximity to Sicily meant it was vulnerable to air attack. Until the mid-1930s, Malta was virtually undefended, and senior Royal Navy officers did not believe it could be held in the event of war. To supply Malta, convoys from Gibraltar or Alexandria had to run the gauntlet of the Regia Marina and land-based aircraft. The Royal Navy did not dare send its battleships and carriers all the way to Malta, and the last part of the journey had to be accomplished without heavy escort.

After German forces joined the Western Desert battle over the Suez Canal in January 1941, the supply route from Italy to North African ports and likewise the Allies' need to supply Malta became the focus for engagements. The Italian fleet anchorage at Taranto in the 'heel' of Italy was ideally situated for attacks on the Alexandria–Malta route.

Royal Navy losses in the eastern Mediterranean during the Battle of Crete in May 1941 fundamentally weakened British naval forces in the region, and in particular heavy damage to HMS *Formidable* put an end to a fleet carrier being permanently stationed there until 1943, reducing opportunities for torpedo strikes against Regia Marina warships. Later in the war, mounting fuel shortages for both German and Italian navies increasingly confined heavy warships to port.

Having just flown over the plane guard destroyer HMS *Wheatland*, an Albacore torpedo-bomber closes on the stern of *Formidable* prior to landing back on board. The second of the new Illustrious-class armoured carriers, *Formidable*'s arrival in the Mediterranean in March 1941 allowed carrier operations to take place in-theatre even with the degree of risk posed by land-based aircraft from August 1940. (Author's Collection)

THE COMBATANTS

TORPEDO-BOMBER AIRCREW

Each Fleet Air Arm torpedo-bomber crew was made up of a pilot, Observer and TAG. Early in the war, the Fleet Air Arm was short of aircrew and worked to recruit from within its own ranks and from outside. For a time, new entrants who had passed their naval officer exams were only accepted if they agreed to go into aircrew training, rather than general service, being given the choice of pilot or Observer. The Royal Navy stopped accepting regular applicants and took new entrants on a 'hostilities only' basis, due to the sheer number of recruits compared with the peacetime navy, and numbers increased as the Fleet Air Arm expanded throughout the war. The makeup of torpedo-bomber aircrew therefore changed from substantially regular personnel at the outbreak of war to mostly volunteers at the end. Furthermore, an increasing number of entrants came from the dominions, particularly New Zealand.

All Fleet Air Arm trainee aircrews, even those who joined as future officers, would begin with the rank of Airman 2nd Class and conduct the same 'squarebashing' that naval ratings underwent. They would move on to training more specific to their role – flying training for pilots, navigation for Observers and gunnery and radio operation for TAGs.

Pilots passing their training would be assigned to either strike aircraft or fighters depending on which they were best suited to. Pilots and Observers were mostly, though not all, officers. The latter were trained chiefly in navigation, as this was their primary role, but other aspects included wireless telegraphy and air gunnery, as they covered these roles in the absence of a TAG. Officers would then undertake a 'knife and fork' course to instruct them in the business of being a naval officer.

On completing their training, Observers and pilots would receive the rank of Midshipman if they were under 21, or otherwise Sub-Lieutenant. Naval ratings could train as pilots or Observers and would on qualification become Petty Officer Pilot or Rating Observer, respectively. The latter were relatively rare, due to the Royal Navy seeing the Observer as the more important role.

TAGs were naval ratings trained as gunners and radio operators to free up Observers for navigating. Training included air-gunnery, initially on the ground and then in the air, firing at towed drogues and fixed targets on land or sea. They were also trained to operate radio equipment, including beacon navigation.

Aircrew from 832 NAS in June 1941 with one of their Albacore torpedo-bombers, two months after the squadron formed. Most of those with visible rank insignia are sub-lieutenants from the Royal Naval Volunteer Reserve with their 'wavy' insignia stripes. The exception is an 'Air Branch' sub-lieutenant, as indicated by the regular Royal Navy sleeve insignia with 'A' in the loop. Sub Lt Peter Sayer, fifth from left, was killed shortly after his wedding during a sortie off Norway from *Victorious* on 23 October 1941. (David McNaught)

Aircrew who passed this stage of their training would go on to a second-line TSR training squadron before assignment to an operational unit. Personnel were encouraged to form regular crews who would fly together at all times, and stay together as long as circumstances allowed, even when changing squadrons.

Derrik Armson, who flew with 822 NAS, volunteered for the Fleet Air Arm from the surface navy. He described the torpedo-bomber pilot's basic training process during a conversation with the author in 2011:

We thought that they would give us torpedoes and that would be it. But what happened was we had to learn to fly with this quite heavy concrete 'block' on, fly low and all the rest of it. When they were satisfied we were confident enough we were given torpedoes, real ones, except instead of having an explosive charge on the head, they had a smoke canister.

The torpedo was set to run at a height, or a depth I should say, below the ship that we were aiming at – we didn't want to hit the ship, obviously, and they didn't want to lose the torpedo, which was a very expensive bit of equipment. Anyway, once we'd finished our job and dropped them, they ran below the water. If you dropped them to splash, the back of the torpedo could easily break and they'd just sink. If you dropped them with the nose of the aircraft slightly down, they went straight into the water at an angle and plummeted down before gradually coming back up again. If you dropped them too nose-up and they didn't break, they just went along the surface of the water like a steamboat, and you just had to hope you didn't hit the ship.

Cdr 'Bertie' Vigrass flew Swordfish and Barracudas in the torpedo role. He described how pilots would learn to drop a torpedo accurately during a conversation with the author in 2013:

Fleet Air Arm aircrew in training observe a torpedo being loaded onto an Albacore. The aircraft's torpedo sight – the curved, 'toothed' rail in front of the cockpit – is clearly visible. (Author's Collection)

Our aim was to drop the torpedo 1,000 yards from the target, at 50ft and at 86 knots, flying level, with no 'skid' on the aircraft, as the rear of the torpedo was released slightly later than the nose of the torpedo in order to create a nose-down attitude (for a correct entry into the sea). Any 'skid' on the aircraft would have deflected the torpedo from a satisfactory entry into the sea.

If the captain of the ship was well trained he could 'comb' the torpedo – turn towards it – and it would then pass ahead of the ship. We would always try to cause the captain to commit the ship to a turn before we dropped our torpedo, and we could then adjust our 'lay-off' accordingly.

There were no aids to assist the pilot in assessing the range from the target or the aircraft height – only the experience of the pilot. We practised constantly on friendly 'targets', and we had a camera that recorded our dive and which stopped when we would have dropped the torpedo, had we been carrying one. From the film it was possible to assess the accuracy and the result of the 'attack'.

AXIS ANTI-AIRCRAFT GUNNERS

The Kriegsmarine trained anti-aircraft gunners as part of its overall gunnery training programme. Ratings could specialise in anti-aircraft gunnery, with grades including Geschützführer, Flak (Chief gun captain, Flak), Flak-Entfernungsmesser (anti-aircraft fire-controlman – rangefinder operator), Flak-Maschinenwaffenführer (anti-aircraft machine gun crew leader) and Flak-Maschinenwaffenschütze (anti-aircraft machine gunner).

A senior officer instructs Kriegsmarine gunnery cadets aboard *Bremse*, one of two dedicated gunnery training ships in the German navy. Crewmen were also taught anti-aircraft gunnery whilst embarked in the vessel. (Author's Collection)

The Kriegsmarine built two dedicated gunnery training ships in the interwar period, *Bremse* and *Brummer*. The former was designed to fit four 2cm/65 Flak 30 guns and four 3.7cm SKC/30, although the latter were not fitted until 1941, along with an additional four 2cm guns. During peacetime it could accommodate 90 trainee gunners. The larger *Brummer* was more focused on anti-aircraft gunnery training, being fitted with two twin 10.5cm SKC/33, one twin 8.8cm SKC/35, two twin 3.7cm SKC/30 and two single 2cm C/30 guns. It accommodated 298 cadets. Both vessels did much to develop the wartime core of anti-aircraft gunners. Training was thorough and produced effective crews.

The Kriegsmarine did not have a formal process of awarding 'kills' to anti-aircraft gunners, but in special cases good performance could be recognised. One such was Bootsmannsmaat (Boatswain's Mate) Karl Jörss, awarded the Knight's Cross on 23 February 1943. Jörss' citation noted that 'He excelled in repelling numerous air attacks. By skilful fire control he managed to repel all attacks, to save the ships and their cargoes from being destroyed, with 12 observed kills'.

Part of the crew of a twin 3.7cm SKC/30 medium Flak gun on board the mine-barrage breaking vessel *Sperrbrecher 16*. This mounting was normally manned by six personnel, plus ammunition passers. (Author's Collection)

Training and experience was paramount, and lack of it could weaken a ship's defence. *Bismarck*'s anti-aircraft gunners had had little opportunity to practise or learn the particular quirks of their ship before embarking on Operation *Rheinübung*. The Flak divisions aboard *Bismarck* numbered 360 men.

The interrogation of survivors from the vessel revealed a considerable amount about the manning of Flak batteries. Regarding the 10.5cm guns, 'The gun's crew for the twin mountings (excluding ammunition supply) consisted of 12 men, led by the "Geschuessführer" (captain of the gun), who was either a

SIR ARTHUR LUMLEY LYSTER

The officer known to all as Lumley Lyster started his career in the Royal Navy as a proponent of the big-gun battleship, but between the wars he began to champion naval aviation.

Lyster had joined the Royal Navy in 1901 and specialised in gunnery. His postings took him from Gunnery Officer on a light cruiser in 1917, to Squadron Gunnery Officer of a battleship squadron in 1922, to the Admiralty's Ordnance Committee in 1928, to Captain of Chatham Gunnery School in 1935. During World War I, however, Lyster was seconded to the Italian Fleet with Wg Cdr Arthur Longmore, where they set up a seaplane unit at Taranto. Twenty years later, Lyster returned to the Mediterranean and naval aviation when he was appointed captain of HMS *Glorious*. One of the carrier's officers described Lyster as 'the ideal choice to command our combined service unit of RAF, Royal Navy and Royal Marines' – British carriers retained many RAF personnel into World War II.

In 1935, Italy invaded Abyssinia, triggering fears that Mussolini might launch an unprovoked attack on the Royal Navy. The Mediterranean Fleet drew up plans to target the Regia Marina's fleet anchorage at Taranto, but the threat receded when it became clear that the League of Nations would take no action against Italy.

In 1938 (the year after Lyster took command of *Glorious*) the German occupation of Czechoslovakia heightened tensions once again, while Hitler and Mussolini had signed a protocol establishing the Axis. Admiral Sir Dudley Pound, then Commander-in-Chief in the Mediterranean, charged Lyster with updating the plan to attack Taranto, taking advantage of his knowledge of the base from 1917.

Lyster instituted training in night flying and torpedo attacks on static targets close inshore, using Grand Harbour in Malta as an analogue for Taranto. After intensive training, Lyster was convinced that an attack could be successfully

Vice-Admiral Sir Arthur Lumley Lyster. (Author's Collection)

mounted. He was promoted to flag rank in 1939, and the following year appointed to oversee the aircraft carriers in the Mediterranean. It was natural that he would resurrect the plans to strike at the heart of the Regia Marina by air, especially as Pound was now First Sea Lord and fully backed such a strategy. Lyster's next task was to fine-tune the plans and work up the air groups of *Eagle* and *Illustrious*. In this, he succeeded brilliantly.

Lyster continued to excel at leading the Royal Navy's carrier operations throughout the war, with further successes including the vital Malta convoys of mid-1942, in which carrier air power played a vital role. His final wartime posting, appropriately enough, was as flag officer in charge of carrier training.

"Bootsmaat" or "Oberbootsmaat" (petty officer, 2nd or 1st class)'. Within the crew was a range setter, three deflection setters, a gunlayer, a trainer, a fuse-setter (in constant radio contact with the plotting room), a fuse correction setter, two loaders and a firer.

There was a clear hierarchy for control of the anti-aircraft defences on Kriegsmarine capital ships, as revealed by interrogation of *Bismarck* survivors. They described officers and their roles, as well as the relationship between batteries. Kapitänleutnant

ERICH RAEDER

Erich Raeder was the architect of Germany's efforts to rebuild a battle fleet from scratch, and consequently the reason the Fleet Air Arm had to face several powerful, well-protected German warships. He also led the Kriegsmarine when those warships were most active.

Raeder joined Imperial Germany's Kaiserliche Marine as a cadet in 1894, and he immediately impressed his superiors. During World War I he was chief of staff to Admiral Franz Ritter von Hipper, the commanding officer of the German battlecruisers. After the war he supported the unsuccessful Kapp Putsch which aimed to overthrow the Weimar Republic in favour of autocratic government. Raeder spent two years sidelined, but a scandal in 1928 forced many senior officers out and created an opening at the head of the Reichsmarine.

Raeder modelled himself on Großdmiral Alfred von Tirpitz, creator of the World War I battle fleet. He agitated for Germany to repudiate the Versailles Treaty and begin to rearm. After a new government was elected on a platform of cancelling the new *panzerschiffe*, he persuaded them to retain the construction programme.

The Versailles Treaty left Germany without major modern warships. The resources required to build a competitive, conventional battle fleet were formidable. Almost singlehandedly, Raeder overcame the dominance of the army in German military planning. While Hitler hoped to avoid contact with the major naval powers, Raeder persuaded him that building a powerful navy could deter those countries from challenging Germany. He defeated the voices calling for more practical but less ambitious strategies of cruiser or submarine warfare, and secured funding for a powerful conventional fleet.

On the outbreak of war in September 1939, Raeder was faced with an incomplete plan and an unbalanced force that was not ideal for cruiser (raider) warfare and completely inadequate to fight a fleet action against a major power. He was therefore pushed into adopting the former in the hope that the resulting dispersal of Allied naval forces would erode their strength.

Successful raider actions from 1939 to 1941 showed promise, although securing Hitler's agreement to release major warships for these operations was a constant challenge. When Raeder initiated Operation *Rheinübung* – the commerce raiding operation by the battleship *Bismarck*

Großadmiral Erich Raeder. (Author's Collection)

and cruiser *Prinz Eugen* – without Hitler's approval, he was gambling on its success. Instead, the loss of the battleship seemed to confirm Hitler's fears about the risks to major warships. Raeder hung onto his role, but his influence over Hitler was fatally damaged. Late that year, Hitler pressed for the heavy warships at Brest to be brought to Norway. The resulting Operation *Cerberus*, planned by Raeder in spite of his own reservations, was a success on its own terms, but removed a threat to Atlantic convoys.

There was still the possibility of operations against Russian convoys, but a mix of Hitler's indecisiveness, bad luck, increasing fuel shortages and heavy Royal Navy escorts made success elusive. Raeder's final error was to report the Battle of the Barents Sea on 31 December 1942 as a victory for the Kriegsmarine. In fact, although several warships had been sunk or damaged, all the merchant ships in the convoy they were escorting arrived unscathed. Hitler, furious, ordered that Raeder's heavy warships be scrapped, and rather than carry out the order, Raeder resigned.

Gellert was 'In charge of all "Flak" weapons', while other 'Flakleiters' commanded a portion of the defences such as aft long-range or forward close-range weapons. Oberleutnant-zur-See Jürgen Brandes controlled all close-range weapons from a position at the foot of the mainmast, while Oberleutnant-zur-See Soltau controlled the short range anti-aircraft guns forward from the gallery below the upper forward director tower.

The Regia Marina traditionally took gunnery very seriously, although training, particularly in anti-aircraft fire, was hampered from the outbreak of war due to shortages. A practice shoot with anti-aircraft guns was recorded by *Conte di Cavour* and *Cesare* in May 1940, but it is not clear how regular a process this was.

Writer Enrico Cernuschi had an uncle who served in the Regia Marina during World War II. He recalled that by 1942, training 'was purely theoretical. At the Scuola Mitraglieri at Pola in 1942, my uncle remembered the sailors were allowed to fire two clips only before being considered combat ready and sent to the ships. The problem was, since June 1940, the lack of anti-aircraft shells, which caused the immediate order to fire only "con puntamento a vista" – i.e. aiming at the aircraft, when sighted, with no barrage fire'.

'Kill' markings for a single 3.7cm SKC/30 gun on board a Kriegsmarine escort vessel, indicating three Soviet aircraft shot down – two twin-engined and one single-engined. (Author's Collection)

This was less of an issue for cruisers and battleships, which had sophisticated fire-control systems. However, destroyers in the outer screen for the battle fleet did not have anti-aircraft directors, and typically used barrage fire (relying on sheer weight of fire rather than accuracy) for protection.

A Regia Marina anti-aircraft gunner at a 100mm/47 OTO Model 1928 gun aboard a cruiser in November 1942. He is in intercom contact with the director to provide information such as target bearing, speed and wind-speed, as well as reporting back the accuracy of shell bursts. (Author's Collection)

COMBAT

NORWAY

Furious was the first carrier on station when German forces invaded Norway in April 1940, with Swordfish-equipped 816 and 818 NASs embarked. The following morning, *Furious* launched its Swordfish with torpedoes to attack Kriegsmarine destroyers in Trondheimsfjord after they had transported mountain troops to seize Trondheim. Aircraft from 816 NAS attacked *Theodor Riedel,* but it had been deliberately beached to provide gunfire support to the troops ashore, and the torpedoes all grounded in the sand. Swordfish from 818 NAS found another destroyer underway, although it was close enough inshore that high ground hampered the aircrafts' approach. Nevertheless, crews claimed a possible hit, although this was unlikely.

The experience showed that a torpedo attack inshore was reliant on good intelligence of the locale. Thereafter, much effort went into reconnaissance and information gathering about the site of any potential attack. There were few further opportunities for torpedo attack during the Norwegian campaign, which ended ignominiously for the Allies in early June. Attrition had reduced the number of Swordfish in frontline use at that time to 75 – a serious matter, considering there would be no replacements for another six months. *Glorious* was sunk by the battleships *Scharnhorst* and *Gneisenau* during the withdrawal, without launching a single Swordfish to hit back, leading to the loss of six 823 NAS aircraft. The other half of the squadron was ashore at Hatston, in the Orkneys.

Scharnhorst put into Trondheim with damage from the engagement. On 20 June temporary repairs allowed it to head south with six escorts to Kiel, where the warship was to be dry-docked. The vessels were spotted by an RAF Hudson off Sognefjordan the following day, and the Royal Navy quickly realised that the warships would soon

be in range of Swordfish flying from Hatston . . . just. A handful of the torpedo-bombers were available from two under-strength squadrons – 823 NAS, which had lost half of its aircraft with the sinking of *Glorious*, and 821 NAS, disembarked from *Ark Royal*.

Many of the crews were inexperienced and badly in need of more training, especially in torpedo attack. Six aircraft were scraped together, three from each squadron, and sent out. In many respects, the crews involved displayed considerable skill – their navigation was perfect, intercepting the ships at the point of minimum distance, 240 miles from Hatston, avoiding a wasteful search.

Just after 1600 hrs on 21 June, the destroyer *Steinbrinck* reported six aircraft approaching at low level from the east. *Scharnhorst* and its escorts put up a fearsome anti-aircraft barrage, but the Swordfish pressed home their attack through the fire. Here, though, the lack of preparation in anti-ship missions told, and the aircrews failed to split up their attack runs or vary their direction of approach. All the torpedoes were dropped on the same side, allowing *Scharnhorst* to comb them easily. Two of the Swordfish were brought down by the ships' anti-aircraft batteries, both from 823 NAS.

One of the returning aircraft had only seven gallons of fuel remaining, demonstrating how small margins were. Even so, with better preparation, the Swordfish might have found more success, but the previous few months had eroded the strength and skill of the Fleet Air Arm's torpedo-bomber squadrons.

THE MEDITERRANEAN

Following Mussolini's declaration of war on Britain and France on 10 June 1940, *Ark Royal* was sent to the Mediterranean to take up station in the western end with Force H at Gibraltar. Covering the eastern end was the old carrier *Eagle*, based at Alexandria. Pre-war planning assumed that the French Navy would take the lead in the western Mediterranean, but France was already on the brink of defeat.

The first successful attacks on major warships by Fleet Air Arm torpedo-bombers during World War II were, therefore, not against Axis vessels but French warships at Mers-el-Kébir, in French Algeria, and Dakar, in French West Africa, when their crews resisted Royal Navy demands that they disarm. *Dunkerque* was severely damaged by *Ark Royal*'s Swordfish on 6 July, and two days later the battleship *Richelieu* at Dakar suffered a similar fate at the hands of aircraft from HMS *Hermes*.

While this was taking place, the Mediterranean Fleet at Alexandria learned an Italian convoy had put into Tobruk, on the Libyan coast. Reconnaissance on 5 July revealed seven destroyers, six merchantmen and numerous smaller escort vessels in port. *Eagle* disembarked nine Swordfish ashore at Sidi Barrani, on the Egyptian coast, from where they set off, aiming to hit the ships in harbour at dusk.

Despite plenty of warning that an attack was coming from the earlier reconnaissance flights, the Swordfish arrived with complete surprise. Lt Cdr Nicholas Kennedy, the commanding officer of 813 NAS, attacked the destroyer *Zeffiro* at point-black range, his torpedo detonating the ship's magazine and breaking its back. The destroyer *Euro* was also hit and had to be beached to stop it sinking. A merchantman was sunk and two more damaged.

The success of torpedo attacks against ships in port would set a pattern for the Fleet Air Arm for the rest of the year. Its Swordfish squadrons in the Mediterranean would spend much time and effort developing the requisite skills and tactics, culminating in the attack on Taranto in November. Before that though, the Swordfish would finally take part in a fleet engagement in open sea.

On 9 July, the Italian and British battle fleets were each supporting a convoy across the eastern Mediterranean. A British destroyer spotted two Regia Marina battleships and *Eagle* flew off several Swordfish to pinpoint the opposing fleet. The shortcomings of only having a single carrier, and a small one at that, hampered the Royal Navy as *Eagle* was unable to maintain a shadower on station and launch a strike at the same time. The Italian fleet changed course while the strike Swordfish were on their way, resulting in the aircraft failing to find the battleships. They did find another group of cruisers at 1330 hrs and attacked, without success.

The Navigatori-class warship *Leone Pancaldo* of 1929 was initially an 'esploratore' (flotilla leader/scout cruiser) before being re-rated as a destroyer in 1938, despite being considerably larger than most vessels of that type – it weighed 2,621 tons when fully loaded. Although the destroyer was sunk at anchor in Augusta harbour by Swordfish from *Eagle* on 9 July 1940, it was subsequently re-floated on 26 July 1941 and returned to service on 12 December 1942. *Leone Pancaldo* was sunk by Allied air attack for a second time on 30 April 1943. (Author's Collection)

A second strike a few hours later located the battleships again, but the flight leader mistook the cruiser *Bolzano* for a battleship and all aircraft attacked it, again without success, despite the strike being described by the leader as 'very well executed and pressed well home'. The Commander-in-Chief, Vice-Admiral Sir Andrew Cunningham, called off the action (later known as the Battle of Calabria) before a third strike could be flown off. Cunningham expressed disappointment in the Swordfish attacks, while accepting that the pilots had not had much opportunity for practice, and praised efforts to provide strike, anti-submarine and reconnaissance sorties with only one carrier and 17 Swordfish.

Circumstances threw *Eagle* a second chance, however. Reconnaissance revealed that two Regia Marina cruisers and six destroyers had put into Augusta, Sicily, to refuel. These vessels were within reach of *Eagle*'s aircraft, and Lt Cdr Kennedy led nine Swordfish across the Malta Channel at dusk on the 10th. Just after sunset at 2023 hrs, Kennedy, flying E4A, directed the aircraft to split into three flights, leading his own group at low-level right into the harbour mouth.

In the meantime, however, the Regia Marina had intercepted radio communications about the strike, so most of the fleet had left. Only two large Navigatori-class destroyers were present when the Swordfish arrived. One, *Leone Pancaldo*, had finished refuelling a little earlier and was anchored in the middle of the harbour. The other, *Ugolino Vivaldi*, was tied up at the mole, still refuelling. In the gloom, Kennedy misidentified *Vivaldi* as an oiler. He launched his torpedo at *Leone Pancaldo* and saw an explosion, thinking he had sunk the destroyer. His torpedo had in fact passed astern of the vessel and struck a reef.

The second aircraft from Kennedy's section, E4B flown by Lt K. L. Keith, targeted *Vivaldi*, but his torpedo ran into shallow water and grounded. Lt D. N. Collins in the second section aimed at *Leone Pancaldo* and hit it, the torpedo striking the bow at the forward boiler room. The flooding was catastrophic and within a few minutes the water had reached the superstructure. The destroyer's captain ordered the crew to abandon ship, and less than a quarter of an hour after the attack began, *Leone Pancaldo* had been sunk.

Two more aircraft attempted to torpedo *Vivaldi*, but missed, and the rest, seeing no targets, returned to Malta with their torpedoes. The anti-aircraft defences only started up in earnest as the Swordfish were leaving.

Although the results were less than had been hoped for, the attack proved that ships could be successfully targeted in harbour at night. Nocturnal operations mitigated some of the weaknesses of the Swordfish, such as its low speed and lack of protection, while playing to its strengths. *Eagle* returned to port after the strike on Augusta and disembarked its aircraft.

It was believed that the cruiser *Giovanni delle Bande Nere* had put into Tobruk on 20 July after having been damaged in action with Royal Navy cruisers, so a raid was staged by 824 NAS, taking advantage of a moonlit night. In fact, the cruiser had gone to Benghazi, further west along the Libyan coast, but several destroyers and auxiliary vessels were present. This time, the defences were awake when the Swordfish arrived at 2230 hrs, and heavy anti-aircraft fire prevented crews from identifying targets for several hours – their cause was not helped by cloud over the target. Finally, the Swordfish worked into an attack position at around 0130 hrs and torpedoed the destroyers *Nembo* and *Ostro* and the merchantman *Sereno*, sinking all three.

Eagle was due to take part in a cruise with other warships of the fleet in the eastern Mediterranean in August, but the battleship HMS *Malaya* developed faults with its machinery and the operation was postponed. Instead, the carrier disembarked its aircraft to Dekheila, in Alexandria, with orders to respond to RAF reconnaissance reports of enemy shipping off the coast of Libya.

One such report was received on the morning of 22 August after a destroyer, submarines and depot ships were spotted near Ain-el-Gazala, in the Gulf of Bomba. A strike of three Swordfish led by Royal Marine Capt Oliver Patch was launched at 1038 hrs. The aircraft reached the coast in the correct area just over two hours later and found the large submarine Iride alongside the support vessel *Monte Gargano*, with other ships beyond.

Italian corvettes in Augusta harbour on Sicily, where Italian cruisers and destroyers refuelled after the Battle of Calabria. The vessels' presence prompted a raid by Fleet Air Arm Swordfish on 9 July 1940, although in the event only two destroyers were still there when the aircraft arrived. (Author's Collection)

The Swordfish split up, the leader going straight for the submarine while the other two aircraft swung round to attack the ships behind it. Patch dropped his torpedo 300 yards from Iride, resulting in a direct hit. The submarine immediately broke in two and sank. Another Swordfish launched a torpedo at *Monte Gargano* and sank it, while the Spica-class torpedo boat *Calipso* was damaged. The Swordfish crews believed they had actually destroyed four ships with three torpedoes, and much publicity was made of this.

While only two vessels were sunk, the strike had achieved a greater success than the Royal Navy could have imagined. Iride was carrying the first operational example of a 'human torpedo', as well as its crew and support equipment, preparing for an attack on warships in Alexandria. With the loss of the submarine, the Regia Marina was not able to mount such an attack until December 1941. Had the planned raid been successful in the autumn of 1940, it could have drastically affected the balance of power in the Mediterranean against the Allies.

TARANTO

The next shift of naval power in the theatre would be in the Allies' favour. All the lessons and experience from the previous raids on warships in port culminated in Operation *Judgement*, the raid on the Italian battle fleet anchorage at Taranto.

The idea was not new. During the Abyssinian Crisis, plans for a raid on the Italian fleet at Taranto had been drawn up and the torpedo squadrons trained. When war was declared in September 1939, it was likely to be only a matter of time before hostilities commenced against Italy. The First Sea Lord, Admiral of the Fleet Sir Dudley Pound, wrote 'I think there is a great deal to be said for making an attack by air on the Italian fleet at Taranto. One reason for this is that I do not believe *Glorious* will be able to remain in a serviceable condition in the Mediterranean for very long, what with air and submarine attack, and it may be a good thing to get

Illustrious launches Swordfish near its 'chummy ship', the battleship *Warspite*, after the carrier had joined the Mediterranean Fleet in September 1940. (Author's Collection)

the most one can out of her before she is placed *hors de combat*'.

This is a sobering insight into the Admiralty's expectations for the survivability of a carrier in the Mediterranean. *Glorious* was lost even before she could return to the Mediterranean, but the idea remained. In August 1940, its former captain, Sir Arthur Lyster, returned to the Mediterranean as Rear Admiral, Aircraft Carriers, flying his flag aboard *Illustrious*.

For all the efforts to develop the science of targeting warships in port at night, the means for a successful attack on Taranto were not fully in place until late 1940. Previous raids going back to Norway emphasised the need for detailed and up-to-date reconnaissance, and it was only with the arrival of the American-built Martin Maryland on Malta that British forces had an aircraft fast enough to reconnoitre the harbour at Taranto and escape with the information. Internal long-range fuel tanks for the Swordfish that extended their range to 600 miles were only recently available too. Without these, the carriers would struggle to reach the flying off point without detection. With *Illustrious* joining *Eagle*, a large enough force was present by the autumn of 1940 to seriously consider such an attack.

The Marylands soon brought back photographs showing the port's defences in detail. There were 101 anti-aircraft guns ashore, divided across 21 batteries, 84 heavy machine guns and 109 light machine guns. To this could be added the anti-aircraft defences of all the ships at anchor, booms and torpedo nets, 87 tethered barrage balloons and 22 searchlights. An early warning system with 13 sound detectors could give advance warning of an attack.

On paper, the defences at Taranto were formidable. In reality though, Taranto was vulnerable. The inner harbour, Mar Piccolo, was too small and shallow for a torpedo attack, but only cruisers and destroyers were anchored there as the battleships were too big to enter. The larger ships were anchored in the much more open outer harbour, Mar Grande. Some of the shore-based anti-aircraft guns were obsolete. In autumn storms, 60 of the barrage balloons blew away and there was insufficient hydrogen to replace them for some time. The torpedo nets, at a depth of ten metres, did not extend below the maximum draught of the battleships at anchor, and while 4,200m of nets were in place, this was only a third of what the Regia Marina deemed necessary – no more netting was yet available. Finally, the sound detectors were unable to pick up aircraft approaching at low-level.

However, problems with both carriers put the raid in jeopardy. A fire in *Illustrious'* hangar put an end to hopes of a Trafalgar Day (21 October) attack, and the raid had to be rescheduled for the next favourable phase of the moon. Then, *Eagle*, its ageing hull shaken by numerous bomb near-misses, developed faults in its aviation fuel systems that needed dockyard attention to put right. Contamination of aircraft fuel on board *Illustrious* led to the loss of three Swordfish.

The decision was taken to go ahead despite these setbacks, transferring as many aircraft as possible from *Eagle* to *Illustrious*. It was felt important to include crews from *Eagle*, as their greater experience and high efficiency, gained from months carrying out similar raids, would be invaluable.

The delay did, however, give crews more time to train in flare-dropping. One of the biggest problems with the earlier raids had been identifying targets accurately and directing the attack in darkness. A few aircraft were therefore detailed to drop a string of flares along the shoreline of the anchorage, silhouetting the ships at their moorings for the aircraft approaching from seaward.

On 11 November *Illustrious* reached the launch point, and at 2035 hrs the first aircraft took off. The raid was to consist of 21 aircraft, in two waves, rather than the 30 originally planned. Most Swordfish were armed with torpedoes, while some carried bombs to attack cruisers in the inner harbour and two aircraft in each wave carried flares to illuminate the scene.

The torpedo Swordfish split into two sections as they approached Mar Grande and attacked from slightly different directions, but both arrived at the dropping point at almost exactly 2315 hrs. The flare-dropping aircraft did their job perfectly, and the battleship anchorage was seen in stark relief. An aircraft from the first section launched at *Conte di Cavour*, the southernmost battleship, while the other two appear to have launched at *Andrea Doria*, to the northeast of *Conte di Cavour*, closer to the shoreline. The torpedo aimed at *Conte di Cavour* exploded beneath the hull, below No. 2 main turret, while the other two torpedoes missed and exploded on the bottom. The aircraft that had launched against *Conte di Cavour* was immediately brought down by the guns of that vessel and a nearby destroyer.

The modernised battleship *Andrea Doria* sits in the fleet anchorage at Taranto just before World War II. The vessel is anchored close to where its sister ship *Duilio* was torpedoed by Fleet Air Arm Swordfish on the night of 12–13 November 1940. (Author's Collection)

Jim Laurier

A torpedo detonates against the battleship *Conte di Cavour* at the Italian battle fleet's anchorage at Taranto on the night of 11–12 November 1940. One Swordfish from 815 NAS in the attack's first wave turns away, while the aircraft that scored the hit, 4A, subsequently receives damage from the ship's anti-aircraft batteries, leading to it crashing in the harbour. The barrage balloons protecting part of the anchorage can be seen in the background, and behind that, a string of parachute flares that silhouetted the battleships for the attacking aircraft. Ahead of *Conte di Cavour*, another battleship, *Duilio*, also takes a hit.

The second section attacked from further north, and all three aircraft appear to have launched against *Littorio*, two torpedoes hitting home against the side of the hull. One of these struck to starboard towards the bow, and the other struck the stern to port, the Swordfish in this case having had to make a tight turn back towards the ship after initially passing fairly close astern of it. All but one aircraft of the first wave completed their attacks and turned back for *Illustrious*.

Three-quarters of an hour after the first wave arrived, the second wave of torpedo aircraft reached the target. Apart from one Swordfish which had been delayed, they all attacked in a single group, from a northerly direction, flying over the Tamburi-Lido Azzurro district northwest of the port. In doing so they passed close by the cruiser anchorage to the northwest of the battleships, and one of the Swordfish was shot down, probably by *Gorizia*'s guns. It blew up, killing both crewmen.

From this direction it was inevitable that *Littorio* would be one of the most prominent battleships, and it received another torpedo against the starboard bow. One of the other aircraft successfully dropped at *Duilio*, the northernmost vessel in that part of the anchorage, the torpedo exploding beneath the hull. A solitary Swordfish attacked *Vittorio Veneto*, but its torpedo hit the bottom and exploded without causing any damage.

As the Swordfish left, three severely damaged battleships were struggling to control the flooding. *Conte di Cavour* was the victim of a duplex-pistol torpedo that had exploded beneath the hull, triggered by magnetic influence. The explosion was directly beneath the keel, having bypassed the Pugliese protection in the bilges. Its lethality was exacerbated by shockwaves deflecting off the harbour bed. It ripped a 12m opening in the keel and tore the frame floors open for eight metres. The high-capacity pump room and the forward electrical station were among the spaces quickly flooded, preventing damage control parties from stemming the ingress of water.

Despite *Conte di Cavour*'s captain proposing to run the ship aground, Admiral Bruto Brivonesi, commander of the 5th Naval Division, resisted beaching out of concern that it was so down by the bow that this action might cause the vessel to turn turtle. Efforts to use support ships to pump out the flooding failed, and by the time the decision was taken to beach the battleship, its foredeck was awash. Brivonesi's fears of a capsize were almost realised. On hitting the bottom, *Conte di Cavour* listed to nearly 50 degrees, but as the flooding continued and the stern began to fill, the ship recovered. The vessel finally settled in soft mud with a list of around ten degrees, with only its upperworks above water.

Littorio was Campioni's first priority, and the ship was rapidly moved to a position northeast of the cruiser anchorage where its bow could rest on the bottom. With two torpedo hits forward and large holes torn in the hull, the flooding forward could not be stopped. The hit in the stern was less serious, and although it destroyed the rudder and wrecked the steering gear, the damage inflicted did not lead to catastrophic flooding.

Duilio had been struck by a single torpedo, which, as with the hit to *Conte di Cavour*, had been triggered magnetically under the hull, detonating beneath the keel. This opened the hull for 14.5m on the starboard side and 8.5m on the port. It also had to be beached. Technically, *Duilio* had the least damage of the three ships struck. However, the position of the keel damage meant there was a very real possibility that the battleship could break its back if dry-docked. This led to the need for a specialised caisson to be constructed and manoeuvred into position to reinforce the hull before it could be docked – a complex and time-consuming task.

The cruiser *Trento* and the destroyer *Libeccio*, moored in the Mar Piccolo, had been hit by semi-armour piercing bombs that failed to detonate.

None of the battleships struck at Taranto were beyond repair. However, all required considerable time, effort and resources to make operational again. The fact that three battleships were damaged on one night delayed the repairs overall, as Italy lacked the dockyard facilities to work on all of them at the same time. *Conte di Cavour* would take so long to repair that it was still far from readiness when Italy signed an armistice with the Allies nearly three years later. Furthermore, the work required to repair the damaged battleships absorbed resources and labour that would otherwise have been employed on completing the new battleships under construction, delaying their introduction.

The Battle of Taranto, as the attack became known in British circles, did not have the decisive impact sometimes claimed. The remaining Regia Marina battleships continued to pose a threat to Royal Navy operations. Undoubtedly, though, it tipped the balance in the Royal Navy's favour for months to come, forced the Axis powers to divert resources from other theatres, increased the constraints on Italian admirals in future actions and highlighted the vulnerability of even the most powerful ships to aircraft. As a demonstration of economy of effort it was unparalleled – three battleships had been put out of action for the loss of two aircraft, with the crew of one of them safe.

Later that same month, *Ark Royal*'s aircraft briefly faced two of the remaining three undamaged battleships in the engagement known as the Battle of Cape Spartivento, or the Battaglia di Capo Teulada in Italy. On 27 November, Admiral Inigo Campioni, commanding a force including *Vittorio Veneto* and *Guilio Cesare*, aimed to attack a British convoy sailing from Gibraltar to Alexandria. Force H moved to intercept.

Admiral Sir James Somerville, commanding Force H, and Campioni were constrained by circumstances, the latter by the Italian high command's fear of losing more battleships, resulting in the Regia Marina handling its ships cagily. *Ark Royal* flew off a first strike of 11 Swordfish from 810 NAS at midday, reaching the battleships 40 minutes later. The Swordfish closed to within 1,500ft of the target before the anti-aircraft batteries started firing, and when they did, it was described as 'intense but ill-directed' and 'rather wild'.

Apart from one aircraft which overshot and attacked *Giulio Cesare*, all the Swordfish went for *Vittorio Veneto*. The squadron lacked practice and its aircrews also experienced communication problems, so although the Swordfish made it past the destroyer screen, the attack was uncoordinated and the battleships were able to avoid all torpedoes. The aircrews

The Cavour-class battleship *Giulio Cesare* in port at Naples, loading ahead of a convoy escort operation. Several different anti-aircraft weapons are visible – a twin 37mm cannon by the main turrets, a twin 100mm gun aft of it and two twin 20mm cannon on the upper main turret. The director tower for the anti-aircraft guns can be seen to the right of the main bridge superstructure. (Author's Collection)

believed one torpedo had found its mark, as they saw a column of brown smoke spring up just behind *Vittorio Veneto*'s after funnel. This may have been a misfiring duplex torpedo.

A second strike was flown off but the Italian battleships were by this time withdrawing at high speed, and the leader considered it would take too long to work into position. The Swordfish therefore attacked a more conveniently placed group of cruisers, only to experience the same difficulties as the first strike, and once again no hits were made. The lesson would be learned, and *Ark Royal*'s squadrons would be better practised at torpedo attack the next time they encountered a major warship.

CAPE MATAPAN

The next time Fleet Air Arm torpedo-bombers met the Italian battle fleet it would be at sea in the kind of engagement that was envisaged for the type. Rear Admiral Lyster wrote 'It is considered that the operations of HMS *Formidable* at the Battle of Cape Matapan will remain a standard example of the operations of an aircraft carrier in battle'. *Formidable* had initially joined the Home Fleet, but it was transferred to the Mediterranean to replace sister ship *Illustrious* after that carrier was heavily damaged by the Luftwaffe in January 1941.

For the first time, a Royal Navy carrier would have torpedo-bomber squadrons chiefly equipped with Albacores. These were 826 NAS, the first unit to adopt the type (in March 1940), and 829 NAS. The two units trained and worked up as *Formidable* sailed around the Cape of Good Hope and entered the Mediterranean via the Suez Canal. Numbers of the new aircraft were still tight, and 829 NAS had to make good losses with Swordfish from the reserve held in Egypt.

In March 1941, British codebreakers discovered that the Regia Marina was planning to attack a troopship convoy bringing Allied reinforcements to Greece. The Mediterranean Fleet sailed in secret to intercept the Italians. Despite Vice-Admiral

Albacores of 826 NAS ranged on *Formidable*'s flightdeck at dawn for a strike with bombs. This squadron took part in the Battle of Matapan in March 1941. (Author's Collection)

Cunningham's best efforts, the Regia Marina discovered the presence of British warships at sea, but underestimated the force's strength, and therefore Admiral Angelo Iachino, Commander-in-Chief of the Battle Fleet, continued with his sortie.

On 28 March at 0720 hrs, one of *Formidable*'s patrol aircraft sighted cruisers and destroyers, and a little later another aircraft sighted battleships. The British cruisers raced to close the distance, and just before 1000 hrs, *Formidable* launched a strike of Albacores armed with torpedoes. Two hours later, they sighted the cruiser forces, engaging the vessels just as *Vittorio Veneto* arrived in support of the Italian warships.

As the Albacores dived into the attack, the Royal Navy cruisers found themselves coming under fire from the battleship's 308mm guns. The approach was good, with a classic two-flight attack on either side of the bow, but none of their torpedoes hit. Even so, Iachino was persuaded to open the distance, removing the threat to Cunningham's cruisers. *Formidable* readied a second strike force, although due to the carrier's lack of aircraft, only three Albacores and two Swordfish were available, with two Fairey Fulmars to escort them.

The battleship *Vittorio Veneto* anchoring. The bulge at the vessel's waterline indicates the location of the cylinder for the Pugliese system, which was the ship's key defence against underwater torpedo strikes. (Author's Collection)

The second strike flew off, and after two-and-a-half hours in the air, the lead battleship was sighted. The strike leader, Lt Cdr J. Dalyell-Stead, began working round to attack out of the sun, as the aircraft had not yet been spotted. He entered the dive, and had descended to 5,000ft before the escort vessels' anti-aircraft batteries opened up, while the two Fulmars went in to strafe in an effort to disrupt the gunners. *Vittorio Veneto* began to turn to starboard as the leading three aircraft made their attack, seeing one torpedo apparently hit, though Dalyell-Stead's aircraft was fatally struck by defensive fire. Lt G. M. T. Osborn, leading the sub-flight of two Swordfish, followed, but he found that his slower aircraft were getting left behind. When the battleship began to turn, he realised that he was perfectly placed and attacked on the starboard beam.

The single hit, probably Dalyell-Stead's torpedo, wrecked a propeller shaft, causing heavy flooding and drastically reducing the battleship's speed.

The four surviving aircraft reached *Formidable* at 1600 hrs and landed on. The carrier immediately began preparing a third strike, to be carried out at dusk. The six Albacores and two Swordfish from *Formidable* were to be joined by two Swordfish from 815 NAS, then disembarked at Maleme, on Crete. They reached the Italian fleet at 1840 hrs and found that Iachino had formed his ships into a defensive barricade around the damaged battleship. The anti-aircraft fire from the assembled ships was intense, and a squadron-strength attack was turned away. The only way for the torpedo-bombers to find their way to the target was to split up and try to pick their way through the bombardment.

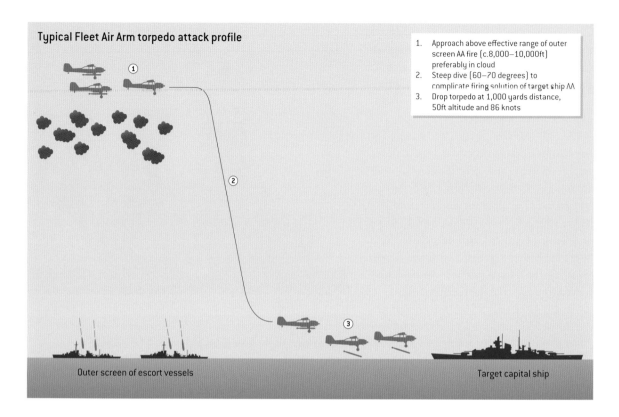

Typical Fleet Air Arm torpedo attack profile

1. Approach above effective range of outer screen AA fire (c.8,000–10,000ft) preferably in cloud
2. Steep dive (60–70 degrees) to complicate firing solution of target ship AA
3. Drop torpedo at 1,000 yards distance, 50ft altitude and 86 knots

Outer screen of escort vessels

Target capital ship

The typical attack profile of Fleet Air Arm torpedo-bombers, approaching at medium altitude to avoid anti-aircraft fire from the target fleet's escort and diving steeply when inside the outer screen to minimise exposure to defensive gunfire. This type of attack was not always possible, with low cloud proving particularly problematic for Swordfish and Albacore aircrew.

By this time it was dark, and searchlight beams were slicing through the sky in all directions. Despite the heavy anti-aircraft fire, all aircrews managed to launch their torpedoes, and most believed they had attacked the *Vittorio Veneto*. In the confusion, and given the similarity in silhouette between Italian battleships and cruisers, it is likely that at least some of the attacks were made against other vessels. All the aircraft proceeded to Maleme rather than attempt to locate and land on *Formidable* in the dark.

Sub Lt G. P. C. Williams was particularly late making his attack, and he reported that the ship he launched at may have been the heavy cruiser *Pola*. He gave his time of attack as 1945 hrs. Despite later claims by Lt F. M. A. Torrens-Spence from 815 NAS that he scored the fatal hit, it is most likely that Williams was the successful pilot based on the time and position of his attack.

Pola had indeed been torpedoed, at 1946 hrs according to its captain, and had stopped dead with no power. The shadowing aircraft reported a ship in this condition, although the Observer was adamant that it was a battleship. *Formidable* was in the line of battle, behind the battleship HMS *Warspite*, and clearly visible from the carrier was a dark form ahead, soon illuminated with searchlights. The carrier's crew were able to see the fruits of their labour at close quarters – Iachino had detached two cruisers and four destroyers to support the damaged *Pola*, not realising the risk from nearby British battleships equipped with radar. The Royal Navy force opened fire and sent *Pola* to the bottom, along with its sister ships *Fiume* and *Zara* and two destroyers.

Vittorio Veneto escaped, despite severe damage to its drivetrain. The outer port propeller had been blown off and the port rudder jammed, while pumps were disabled, leading to an inability to clear the influx of water. As it withdrew, the battleship's stern

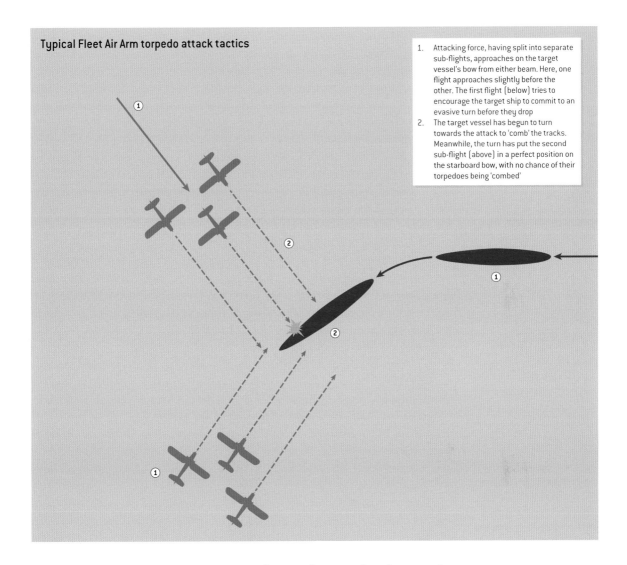

Typical Fleet Air Arm torpedo attack tactics

1. Attacking force, having split into separate sub-flights, approaches on the target vessel's bow from either beam. Here, one flight approaches slightly before the other. The first flight (below) tries to encourage the target ship to commit to an evasive turn before they drop
2. The target vessel has begun to turn towards the attack to 'comb' the tracks. Meanwhile, the turn has put the second sub-flight (above) in a perfect position on the starboard bow, with no chance of their torpedoes being 'combed'

was almost awash. The damage put it out of action for more than four months, reducing the Regia Marina to one modern battleship, only weeks after *Littorio* had returned from its post-Taranto repairs (with *Duilio* not operational until May). The cruiser force was weakened by three of the newest ships in one night, and there were another two destroyers to add to the six already sunk, all thanks to Fleet Air Arm torpedo-bombers.

BISMARCK

In February 1941, *Scharnhorst* and *Gneisenau* passed through the Denmark Strait and began hunting convoys in Operation *Berlin*. The battleships enjoyed a fruitful cruise, with a tally of 22 ships sunk or captured making it the most successful surface raiding mission so far. By March, the Admiralty had little choice but to throw every available resource into protecting convoys, ordering Force H into the Atlantic. *Ark Royal* maintained a constant air search and a torpedo strike force at readiness, including at night, with flares to be used if the battleships were detected during darkness.

The ideal tactics employed by the Fleet Air Arm required an attacking force to split into small units and attack from different directions, preferably on the target ship's bow. The rationale would be that a turn towards one group to 'comb' its torpedoes would render the target ship vulnerable to another group.

Map of the hunt for *Bismarck*, from the battleship's departure from Norway on 21 May 1941 to its eventual sinking six days later. Fleet Air Arm Swordfish torpedo-bombers made two attacks over this period, the decisive one on 26 May, when the vessel was just a few hundred miles from a safe port.

Bismarck is seen down by the bow after taking a shell during the Battle of Denmark Strait on 24 May 1941. The damage it had suffered would be exacerbated a few hours after this photograph was taken when the vessel was struck by a torpedo dropped by a Swordfish from 825 NAS, flying from *Victorious*. The hit slightly slowed the battleship, allowing *Ark Royal*'s Swordfish to deal a more severe blow two days later. (NHHC image NH 69732)

On 20 March, *Gneisenau* captured the tanker *San Casimiro* and despatched it home under prize crew. *Ark Royal*'s aircraft spotted the merchantman and shadowed it, whereupon the prize crew decided to scuttle the tanker. At 1830 hrs, a reconnaissance aircraft returned to the carrier, having spotted *Scharnhorst* and *Gneisenau* an hour before. The strike Swordfish were readied, but *Ark Royal*'s captain considered that they would not be able to attack before dark.

The following morning, a patrol was flown off and Swordfish and Blackburn Skua dive-bombers were readied. This time, the battleships were nowhere to be found, fog hampering the search efforts. By the time they reappeared, they were within 200 miles of the French coast, heading for port. *Ark Royal*'s aircraft had prevented the Kriegsmarine from recovering *San Casimiro*, but another opportunity to attack *Scharnhorst* and *Gneisenau* had been missed. The chance to make up for it, however, would not be long in coming.

On 19 May, *Bismarck* and *Prinz Eugen* departed on Operation *Rheinübung* – a convoy interdiction operation in the Atlantic, which it was hoped would bear as much fruit as Operation *Berlin*. The sortie was intended to be much larger, with support from *Scharnhorst* and *Gneisenau*, but they were unable to take part due to machinery breakdowns and damage from Allied bombing.

Royal Navy efforts to intercept the two warships began immediately, leading to the Battle of Denmark Strait on 24 May when *Bismarck* sunk HMS *Hood* and seriously damaged HMS *Prince of Wales*. Now every available warship was pressed into the search, aiming to stop the battleship before in melted into the expanse of the Atlantic.

The carrier HMS *Victorious* had just joined the Home Fleet, and it was hastily despatched. Its air group was incomplete and not worked up, the torpedo-bomber force comprising only nine Swordfish of 825 NAS. The first operational Swordfish unit had been slowly rebuilding under Lt Cdr E. R. Esmonde after catastrophic losses over Dunkirk.

Victorious came within range of *Bismarck* in the evening of the battle with *Hood*, and launched every available Swordfish. Visibility was poor, and getting worse. In 825 NAS's favour though was a new development – ASV Mk II, an early radar set. Of the nine aircraft, three had ASV, allowing them to pinpoint the battleship. Even so,

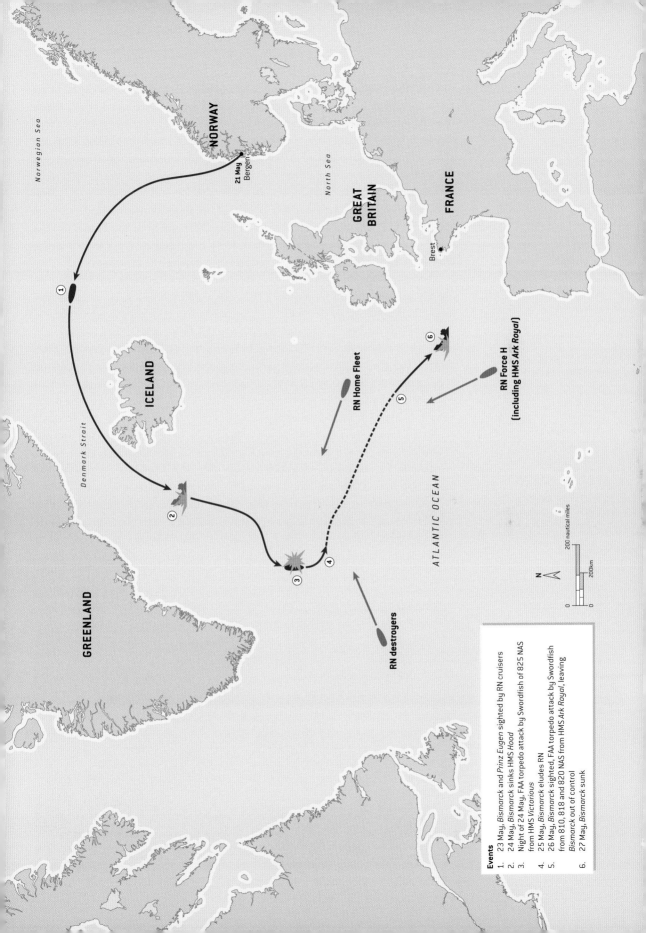

NORWEGIAN Sea

NORWAY

21 May
Bergen

GREAT
BRITAIN

North Sea

FRANCE

Brest

ICELAND

Denmark Strait

GREENLAND

RN Home Fleet

RN Force H
(including HMS *Ark Royal*)

ATLANTIC OCEAN

RN destroyers

N

200 nautical miles

200km

Events

1. 23 May, *Bismarck* and *Prinz Eugen* sighted by RN cruisers
2. 24 May, *Bismarck* sinks HMS *Hood*
3. Night of 24 May, FAA torpedo attack by Swordfish of 825 NAS from HMS *Victorious*
4. 25 May, *Bismarck* eludes RN
5. 26 May, *Bismarck* sighted, FAA torpedo attack by Swordfish from 810, 818 and 820 NAS from HMS *Ark Royal*, leaving *Bismarck* out of control
6. 27 May, *Bismarck* sunk

the thickening cloud presented a challenge, and when Esmonde altered course to get ahead of *Bismarck*, contact was lost. They found the cruiser HMS *Norfolk*, which directed them back towards the target.

The first ASV return, however, turned out not to be *Bismarck* but a US Coastguard cutter which was in the area by coincidence. It was only four miles from *Bismarck*, and when the Swordfish emerged from the cloud, it gave the game away. The battleship's Flak batteries immediately opened up in response.

Although 825 NAS lacked recent experience, its attack showed tactical awareness and skill, and was pressed home with courage. On spotting the battleship, the squadron broke into three sub-flights to deliver a simultaneous attack from multiple directions, giving *Bismarck* a minimal chance of 'combing' the torpedoes.

The ideal torpedo attack according to Fleet Air Arm thinking was for separate flights to converge on either bow, and 825 NAS attempted this, although circumstances meant that each flight delivered its attack separately. Esmonde tried to work round to the starboard bow, but his aircraft took a hit to one aileron, so he elected to go straight in on the port bow. Lt P. D. Gick's flight came in from the starboard side, but Gick aborted, being unsatisfied with the position, and swung round for another attempt, keeping his three aircraft low. The third flight was without one of its aircraft, Sub Lt A. J. Houston having got lost in cloud. Lt H. C. M. Pollard, leading the two remaining Swordfish, aimed at the port quarter.

Bismarck, manoeuvring frantically, avoided all the torpedoes from Esmonde and Pollard's flights, but at that moment Gick and his two companions emerged from the murk on the port bow, launching at close range. One of the three torpedoes struck the battleship's armour belt amidships, sending up 'a towering column of water'.

The successful torpedo appears to have run particularly shallow, possibly even on the surface, and hit the battleship where it was well protected. However, temporary repairs following a shell hit by *Prince of Wales* had failed. Whether this was as a result of the torpedo depressing the armour belt or the vigorous avoiding action loosening

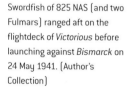

Swordfish of 825 NAS (and two Fulmars) ranged aft on the flightdeck of *Victorious* before launching against *Bismarck* on 24 May 1941. (Author's Collection)

the collision mats, or some combination of the two, flooding had started again and was worse than before. Boiler Room No. 2 had to be abandoned, reducing engine power slightly, and the battleship was trimmed by the bow, both factors reducing its speed.

Bismarck had not escaped unscathed, but neither was it hamstrung. However, any chance of the warship continuing into the Atlantic to carry out a raiding operation was over. The lost fuel and damage meant it would have to put into port. This could mean turning back for Norway or heading southeast towards France, and the Admiralty did not know which. *Bismarck* almost slipped from the Royal Navy's grasp when a misinterpreted radio direction-finding bearing sent the Home Fleet the wrong way, the latter thinking its quarry was heading back into the North Sea. In reality, Brest was the objective. By the time the mistake was realised, the Home Fleet was too far away and too low on fuel to catch *Bismarck* at its current speed. Force H again headed out into the Atlantic from Gibraltar in the hope of cutting off *Bismarck*'s escape.

On the morning of 26 May, an RAF Catalina pinpointed *Bismarck*'s new position, less than 700 miles from Brest. Before too long, it would be under an umbrella of land-based aircraft, but now the battleship was in range of *Ark Royal*, with 810, 818 and 820 NASs' Swordfish on board.

Once again, *Bismarck* was almost handed a lucky break. A failure in communication meant that *Ark Royal*'s first strike mistakenly attacked the cruiser HMS *Sheffield*, which had been shadowing *Bismarck*. Fortunately for *Ark Royal*'s crews, this highlighted a problem with their torpedoes. Several were seen to pass directly beneath the cruiser's hull without exploding, and others detonated as soon as they entered the water. While the magnetic trigger of the duplex pistol had proved successful in previous attacks, there was clearly a problem with it on this occasion.

When the 14 Swordfish returned to *Ark Royal*, their torpedoes were reset to detonate on contact only, and the running depth reduced, balancing a lower chance of severe damage to the battleship's vulnerable keel area against higher reliability. The aim was, after all, not to sink *Bismarck* but to slow it down so the vessel could be caught by battleships, according to Royal Navy doctrine.

It was evening by the time the Swordfish took off again, using *Sheffield* as a signpost, and visibility was even worse than on the 24th. The cloud was too thick to fly around and extended from 700ft to at least 6,000ft, so it was effectively impossible to fly over. Even with the benefit of ASV, the sub-flights became separated in the cloud. Several aircraft found it necessary to emerge from the overcast to check their position, and one group even had to seek out *Sheffield* again for directions. Several aircraft lost their own groups and had to attack with other aircraft that they found, or individually.

The first group to reach the battleship, the sub-flight from 818 NAS led by Lt Cdr T. P. Coode, attacked the port beam, scoring one hit estimated as two-thirds along the waterline. The second group from 810 NAS, led by Lt D. F. Godfrey-Faussett, positioned itself on the starboard beam and was met with 'intense and accurate AA fire'. Sub Lt A. W. D. Beale lost contact with the other aircraft of the flight and had to return to *Sheffield* for a bearing. He found his way back to *Bismarck* and launched a 'determined attack from the port bow in the face of very heavy fire'. His crew reported a hit amidships.

1. Ring gunsight
2. Cockpit coaming padding
3. Lighting switch panel (front to rear – recognition/ navigation lights, landing lamp/pitot head)
4. Radio control switch box
5. Very pistol cartridge holding clips
6. Throttle lever (with press-to-transmit button)
7. Mixture control lever
8. Elevator trim handwheel
9. Inertia starting clutch control ring

10. Inertia starting switch
11. Bomb jettison switch
12. Cockpit light dimmer switch
13. Oil bypass valve control
14. Air intake shutter control
15. Rudder pedals
16. Control column
17. Pilot's seat
18. Boost pressure gauge
19. Priming pump
20. Air pressure gauge
21. Landing lamp deflection control socket
22. Artificial horizon
23. Airspeed indicator

24. Fuel gauge control switch
25. Compass lamp dimmer switch
26. Compass correction card holder
27. Compass lamp
28. Compass
29. Altimeter
30. Torpedo sight control switch
31. Direction indicator (partially obscured by control grip)
32. Turn-and-bank indicator
33. Engine speed indicator
34. Oil temperature gauge
35. Clock

36. Oil pressure gauge
37. Torpedo sight dimmer switch
38. Fuel pressure warning light
39. Starter switch
40. Fuel control cock
41. Downward identification morse key
42. Cockpit light
43. Rudder bias control
44. Rudder bias control lever
45. Brake control lever
46. Automatic boost control cutout
47. VHF radio controller
48. Torpedo sight bars

The next group to attack (from 820 NAS), with Lt H. de G. Hunter leading, descended out of the cloud in time to see the previous sub-flight making its torpedo runs. The 820 NAS Swordfish circled round the stern and launched their own attack on the port side, experiencing heavy anti-aircraft fire that badly damaged one aircraft. Other groups were split up or got lost, finding the anti-aircraft fire too heavy when they arrived. Some launched their torpedoes at extreme range and two jettisoned their weapons.

All the Swordfish made it back to *Ark Royal*, although three were damaged. Aircraft 5B from 818 NAS had splinter damage to its spinner, Townend ring and port lower mainplane, while 2A and 2B from 810 NAS had splinters through the fuselage and port wing, while 4C from 820 NAS was riddled with splinters – 175 holes were counted, including some through the longerons, making the aircraft a write-off. The human casualties were restricted to one pilot with slight wounds to his shoulder and one TAG with a splinter to the thigh.

Upon their return to *Ark Royal*, the aircrews of the strike force were downbeat. They reported two certain hits and one possible, but it did not seem that any real damage had been done. The Swordfish left to shadow the battleship soon revealed the truth. *Bismarck* was out of control, turning two large circles to port and then proceeding north, towards the pursuing warships. One of the torpedoes – possibly that from 818 NAS's Sub Lt J. W. C. Moffat in the first section – had struck the stern and detonated beneath the overhang, deforming the structure and wedging both rudders in a port turn. Numerous attempts were made to free the rudders or find alternative means of steering, but the damage was too severe. Unable to escape, the pursuing battleships caught up and after a lengthy assault with gunfire and torpedoes, *Bismarck* sank.

The torpedo-bombers had fulfilled exactly the role intended for them, hampering an enemy battleship's freedom of manoeuvre and reducing its speed so that the Royal Navy's battleships could deliver the *coup de grace*. The Kriegsmarine's battleship strength had been reduced by 25 per cent for the effective loss of one Swordfish and two crews slightly wounded (plus two Fulmars lost while shadowing). As with Taranto, it had been a striking vindication of the torpedo-bomber's worth.

DECLINE

The heyday of the Fleet Air Arm torpedo-bomber in its primary role against enemy heavy warships was spectacular but relatively brief. The three great triumphs of Taranto, Matapan and *Bismarck* took place over a seven-month period. After that, various circumstances led to fewer opportunities, lower returns and higher losses exacerbated by delays to the Barracuda, and the necessary continuation of obsolete types.

A low point was the attack on Kirkenes and Petsamo in northern Norway on 30 July 1941. The Admiralty was pressured to support the USSR by attacking transport ships in the two ports, from where they supplied German forces on the Murmansk front. Operation *EF* was prepared by Admiral J. C. Tovey, Commander-in-Chief, Home Fleet, despite his misgivings. The ports were close to Luftwaffe airfields, there was no darkness so far north at that time of year and the aircrews of *Victorious* and *Furious* lacked experience in such operations. Tovey

A close formation of Albacores from 786 NAS, a torpedo-bomber training unit based at RNAS Crail, in Scotland, over the sea in early 1941. A high proportion of the Fleet Air Arm's torpedo-bomber crews would be trained at Crail. (Author's Collection)

suggested that attacks on coastal shipping at sea would be preferable, but he was overruled.

Twenty Albacores from *Victorious* were met by Bf 109 and Bf 110 fighters over Kirkenes, and suffered heavy losses as they attempted to torpedo shipping in the harbour. Five aircraft launched their torpedoes at the gunnery training ship *Bremse*, unsuccessfully, and the others attacked transport vessels. Because of the attentions of the fighters, reports on the attacks were confused and the extent of any success hard to judge, although Tovey considered that whatever damage was done, the targets were of low value and did not make up for the losses. Five out of eight Albacores were lost from 828 NAS alone. As it turned out, only two vessels were sunk.

Furious embarked Swordfish and Albacores from 812 and 817 NASs, which found no shipping at Petsamo and expended their ordnance against jetties, quays and oil tanks. Losses from this group were lighter, with only two Fulmar escorts and one torpedo-bomber being lost, but virtually no worthwhile damage was done. Overall, 12 Albacores and four Fulmars had been shot down. Nine aircrew were killed and 27 taken prisoner.

CHANNEL DASH

Scharnhorst and *Gneisenau* were undoubtedly the Bêtes Noires of the Fleet Air Arm, a role they would play again in early 1942. The two battleships were based at Brest after Operation *Berlin*, where they were ideally placed to threaten Atlantic convoys but vulnerable to RAF bombing. By early 1942, they had been damaged several times, taking them out of circulation for raider operations. Meanwhile, Hitler had become paranoid that the Allies planned to invade Norway. He therefore demanded that the ships redeploy there as a deterrent.

The Allies were prepared for this. Operation *Fuller* was drawn up to counter the Kriegsmarine's heavy warships if they sortied, and it included measures to counter a 'dash' through the English Channel with RAF bombers and torpedo-bombers, Royal Navy Motor Torpedo Boats and a small number of Fleet Air Arm torpedo-bombers – six ASV-equipped Swordfish of 825 NAS stationed at Manston, in Kent.

This unit was technically a veteran of the *Bismarck* operation, but half the squadron had been lost with *Ark Royal's* sinking the previous November and it disbanded shortly afterwards. The squadron reformed under the same commanding officer – Lt Cdr Esmonde – in January 1942. It was still in training, with half the squadron at Macrihanish, in Scotland. Esmonde volunteered the six aircraft still at Lee-on-Solent, in Hampshire, to join Operation *Fuller* because of their ability to make a torpedo attack at night, when it was expected that the battleships would attempt to pass through the Channel. Training chiefly consisted of practising night patrols.

Unfortunately, due to mishaps and bad luck, the departure of *Scharnhorst*, *Gneisenau* and *Prinz Eugen* from Brest on 11 February was missed. The force had passed Cherbourg by the time it was noticed, and there were further delays in the Admiralty being notified. Contrary to British expectations, the battleships had not timed their sortie to pass through the narrows off Dover in darkness, instead leaving Brest at night. They were approaching the straits by 1100 hrs, with an escort of destroyers and air cover from Luftwaffe fighters.

The RAF's Bristol Beaufort torpedo-bombers were out of position to attack the vessels, and the available bombers were fitted with the wrong ordnance. The only aircraft capable of attacking in time were the Swordfish at Manston. Esmonde was informed shortly after 1050 hrs, when the warships were detected by the Range and Direction Finding station at Fairlight, in East Sussex. He ordered that the torpedo-bombers be brought to immediate readiness and the torpedoes' running depth to be set for battleships. By the time formal identification was confirmed at 1130 hrs, 825 NAS was well into its preparations.

Vice-Admiral Sir Bertram Ramsay, in charge of the Royal Navy element of Operation *Fuller*, contacted Admiral Dudley Pound, the First Sea Lord, questioning the wisdom of a daylight attack by a handful of obsolete biplanes. Pound responded, 'The Navy will attack the enemy whenever and wherever he is to be found'. This was a death sentence. Even with Pound's words in his ears, Ramsay told Esmonde that as he had not volunteered his squadron for a daylight attack, he was free to withdraw. Esmonde was determined to continue, but pressed the importance of fighter cover.

Strenuous efforts were underway to ensure an escort as the clock ran down. Three squadrons of Spitfires from the Biggin Hill Wing were allocated for top cover, with two more from the Hornchurch Wing as close escort. The rendezvous would have to be at 1225 hrs – any later, and the slow Swordfish might not catch the ships at all. It was soon clear that the fighter squadrons could not fit in briefing, take-off and flight to Manston in the time available, and the RAF informed Esmonde that some or all of the Spitfires would be late. Esmonde waited until 1228 hrs, when a single squadron of ten Spitfires arrived, and set off towards the target.

Within two minutes, the Spitfires were engaged with Fw 190s and Bf 109s, and could not prevent the Swordfish from coming under attack. Before long, they lost touch altogether. Esmonde made it a little beyond the destroyer screen, his aircraft already heavily damaged by fighter attack, and crashed before he could launch his torpedo. The anti-aircraft gunners on *Prinz Eugen* claimed to have shot him down, as did at least one fighter. The remaining two aircraft of the first flight were also damaged from fighter attacks, although they carried on long enough to drop their torpedoes – one at *Prinz Eugen* and the other probably at *Gneisenau* – before they too succumbed to damage and crashed into the sea.

What happened to the three aircraft of the second flight is unclear. One of the crew of the first flight, Observer Sub Lt Edgar Lee, reported seeing them attacking *Prinz Eugen* under heavy anti-aircraft fire. Whether they dropped their torpedoes is not known. Admiral Otto Ciliax, Type Commander, Battleships, who was in charge of the

German vessels, remarked that the 'ancient planes' had been 'piloted by men whose bravery surpasses any other'. It was little consolation.

A board of enquiry concluded that under the circumstances, the decision to send the Swordfish was correct given the importance of slowing down the enemy warships, however remote the chance. Even so, Ramsay later said that had he known only one fighter squadron would turn up, he would have ordered Esmonde to remain on the ground. He recommended Esmonde for the Victoria Cross to add to the Distinguished Service Order he had received following the *Bismarck* action.

But the 'Channel Dash', as it quickly became known, despite being a significant tactical success and a huge propaganda victory for the Kriegsmarine, reduced the threat to Atlantic convoys. According to Großadmiral Raeder, 'The Battle of the Atlantic, as far as our surface forces were concerned, was practically over'. After escaping the Channel, *Scharnhorst* and *Gneisenau* both hit mines, putting them out of action for many months.

Heavy German warships still posed a threat to the Russian convoys, even with *Bismarck* sunk and *Scharnhorst*, *Gneisenau* and *Prinz Eugen* temporarily out of the way (the cruiser torpedoed by a submarine shortly after the Channel Dash). *Tirpitz* was based in Norway, along with *Lützow* (as *Deutschland* had been renamed) and *Admiral Scheer*, making it necessary for the Royal Navy to cover convoys to Russia with heavy escorts, invariably including aircraft carriers.

The month after the Channel Dash, the Kriegsmarine initiated Operation *Sportpalast/Nordmeer*, the first major attempt to strike at the Russian convoys with surface warships. On 1 March, convoy PQ 12 left Iceland for the USSR, while QP 8 departed Murmansk for Iceland. *Tirpitz* sortied from Trondheim with four destroyers five days later, hoping to catch one or both convoys, without being detected by the Allies.

The Home Fleet learned that *Tirpitz* was at sea and mounted a search. The force included *Victorious*, with the Albacores of 817 and 832 NASs, both considered to be well-trained. However, both squadrons had new commanding officers, and Lt Cdr J. W. Lucas, in charge of 832 NAS, had not flown with his new unit at all.

For two days the two groups groped around the North Sea until the Admiralty intercepted a signal locating *Tirpitz*. While the two forces had on occasion been within 100 miles of each other, by the time *Tirpitz* was located, it was too far away for Admiral Tovey's battleships to catch. The only hope was the torpedo-bombers. On the morning of 9 March, *Victorious* launched 12 Albacores loaded with torpedoes, ready to respond when a reconnaissance aircraft located the battleship. The Albacores emerged from the cloud at the battleship's reported position at 0840 hrs and immediately sighted it.

Unfortunately, *Tirpitz* was ahead of the Albacores and steaming upwind, and they found themselves in a stern-chase with the battleship going at full speed. Lucas attempted to conceal the strike force in cloud and overtake the battleship, although with *Tirpitz*'s speed and the wind, the Albacores only gained on their quarry at around 30 knots. Then, the formation flew into a break in the clouds and Lucas considered that he could delay the attack no longer.

The sub-flights became strung out, preventing a coordinated attack. Lucas launched his torpedo as soon as he believed he was in range, attacking on the port bow almost perpendicular to the battleship. The other two flights, meanwhile, positioned themselves to starboard. When Lucas' section attacked, *Tirpitz* turned towards it, combing the torpedoes and placing the other two flights astern, with a low closing speed and under heavy anti-aircraft fire. So much time elapsed between attacks that *Tirpitz* was easily able to reverse the wheel and comb the torpedoes launched to starboard. Two Albacores were shot down by anti-aircraft fire. Later assessment concluded that most aircraft had attacked from much further away than they believed they had, fooled by *Tirpitz*'s size.

One of *Scharnhorst*'s 10.5cm L/31 Flak guns at extreme elevation during a cruise with destroyers, sister ship *Gneisenau* and a Hipper-class cruiser in 1940–41. These guns were replaced with a slightly more advanced mounting, the L/37, before the 'Channel Dash' (Operation *Cerberus*) in February 1942. The nature of the apparent camouflage pattern on the guns is unclear. (Author's Collection)

The failure infuriated Tovey, the Admiralty and Prime Minister Winston Churchill, who demanded to know why not a single hit was made. The consensus was that the attack was poorly executed, and emphasised the importance of training and preparation.

After this, opportunities for torpedo attacks on major warships grew thin. Several fleet carriers were deployed to the western Mediterranean for Malta convoys in 1942, where the main threat was air attack, not surface warships, and the number of torpedo-bombers on carriers was reduced in favour of fighters. Hitler's caution over approving sorties by the Kriegsmarine's heavy warships only grew, while Axis fuel shortages were increasingly acute.

The prominent role played by Royal Navy fleet carriers in the eastern Mediterranean altered after *Formidable* was dive-bombed in May 1941. Thereafter, no fleet carrier was based there until early 1943.

The Royal Navy was at war in the Far East now too, but early brushes with the Imperial Japanese Navy (IJN) demonstrated that the Fleet Air Arm was in no position to challenge. Admiral Sir James Somerville, now Commander-in-Chief, Eastern Fleet, told the Admiralty that he would not be 'subjecting my slow Albacores and Swordfish to so unequal a contest' as a daylight attack in the face of Mitsubishi A6M Zero-sen fighters. Somerville remained on the defensive, hoping that an opportunity for an attack with ASV in poor weather or at night would arise. It did not. Their lordships complained, but there was little that could be done with the obsolete aircraft available.

REBUILDING

In 1943, new monoplane torpedo-bombers began to arrive in squadron service. Barracudas equipped squadrons from January, although it would be many months before the type could be regarded as truly operational. Fleet Air Arm squadrons started to receive Tarpons (Avengers) from June. The Tarpon was considered unsatisfactory as a torpedo-bomber, although it was in demand as an anti-submarine aircraft.

The remaining Fleet Air Arm torpedo-bomber squadrons equipped with Albacores and Swordfish in mid-1943 had received Barracudas or Tarpons by November, while several new units were created from scratch in a period of intense preparation for a new wave of operations. After initial good signs, the work-up of the Barracuda was marred by a series of crashes, many fatal, attributed to mechanical failures and handling issues. Gradually, the problems were resolved or mitigated, and the Barracuda was ready for combat operations by July 1943.

There were two opportunities for the re-equipped torpedo-bomber force to tackle Axis warships. The first was during the Allied landings at Salerno on 9 September 1943, when torpedo-bomber squadrons were embarked on fleet carriers in anticipation of a sortie by the Regia Marina.

Lt 'Bertie' Vigrass, a pilot with Barracuda-equipped 810 NAS embarked in *Illustrious*, said 'They assumed that the Italian fleet would attack us off Salerno, so we did night flying deck landings, practising torpedo dropping, so we would be ready to attack capital ships if we were targeted, which we expected. But on the night before the landings at Salerno, the Italians surrendered, which meant that their fleet didn't come towards us. In fact I spent some time doing anti-submarine patrols round some Italian fleet ships which were about to surrender at Malta'.

Then, on 26 September, *Lützow* was spotted off Gjerøy returning to Kiel from northern Norway. RAF Coastal Command was unable to mount a strike, so responsibility fell to the naval air station at Hatston, and whatever resources it could muster, although the strike would need an RAF escort. Twelve Tarpons were available, manned by experienced crews from 832 NAS. As the Fleet Air Arm did not see the torpedo-bomber role as a primary one for the aircraft, it only had a small stock of US 22.4in. torpedoes. There were just six at Hatston, but, fortunately, the carrier USS *Ranger* (CV-4) had recently joined the Royal Navy's Home Fleet and lent the unit another six.

Maintainers worked through the night preparing aircraft and torpedoes. Early next morning, RAF reconnaissance reported that *Lützow* would pass Stadlandet between 1100 and 1200 hrs. It was expected that the strike would be ordered immediately. However, the officer commanding RAF Coastal Command, Air Marshal Sir John Slessor, refused to allow the Tarpons to take off as he felt there were insufficient escort fighters available. Vice-Admiral Sir Bruce Fraser, Commander-in-Chief Home Fleet, pleaded with Slessor, given the importance of sinking a heavy warship. Slessor relented, and the strike finally took off at 1130 hrs, one hour and 20 minutes late.

Lützow's position was uncertain by now though, and the Tarpons failed to find the warship. It later turned out that they had narrowly missed contact, and had the strike taken place when originally planned they would almost certainly have found their target. Whether it would have translated into a successful attack is a different matter, but given *Lützow*'s relatively weak protection, there was surely a reasonable chance of sinking the ship.

Barracudas carried on the Royal Navy's fight against Axis vessels, but rarely as torpedo-bombers. Dive-bombing raids were carried out against *Tirpitz* in 1944, and the last few torpedo strikes came during an interdiction campaign against German shipping off Norway.

STATISTICS AND ANALYSIS

The Fleet Air Arm estimated that on average, a strike involving 10–12 aircraft against a ship manoeuvring freely should expect one or two torpedo hits. This was achieved in some prominent cases, such as both strikes against *Bismarck* and two strikes at Matapan, but not in others. Rear Admiral D. W. Boyd, the officer commanding aircraft carriers in the Mediterranean in 1941–42, regarded 'only one certain hit from ten aircraft' during the last strike at Matapan as 'disappointing', even though the hit disabled the cruiser *Pola* and led to a significant triumph.

The chances reduced if the target ship had fighter cover. Indeed, when Fleet Air Arm torpedo-bombers occasionally met land-based fighters, they generally suffered heavy losses. Meanwhile, warship anti-aircraft defences were strengthened considerably by major navies from 1941–42, reducing the chances of success without serious losses as at Taranto and against *Bismarck*.

Even earlier in the war, it took immense bravery to press home an attack. After the Battle of Matapan, *Pola*'s commanding officer, Capitano di Vascello *Luigi Corsi,* is reported to have said 'I have never seen such courage as was displayed by the aircraft attacking me. It came in about five feet above the water under a withering fire at short range, and I can only describe it as an act of God'. This echoed comments by Admiral Otto Ciliax during the Channel Dash.

As early as 1940, the Fleet Air Arm's torpedo-bomber strike force sought alternatives to the conventional daylight approach in order to aid survivability. ASV night and poor-weather attacks, and the increasing use of attacks against ships in port, helped address some of the difficulties of attacking at sea.

Swordfish are about to be loaded with running torpedoes for a training flight at a Royal Naval Air Station in 1940–41. These are pre-1940 Fairey-built examples in two different early war colour schemes. Training and experience proved vital to the success of Fleet Air Arm torpedo strikes during World War II. (Author's Collection)

Indeed, the success at Taranto would not have been possible without the earlier raids against ships in harbour at Tobruk, Augusta, Bomba Bay and elsewhere. During these raids, problems such as target identification, illumination and maintaining surprise were noted and solutions developed. The results were spectacular, although recent scholarship has been critical of the failure to reap a decisive result.

A useful comparison can be made with the raids against *Tirpitz* with Barracudas acting as dive-bombers. One lesson learned from these attacks was not to dilute the hitting power of the main striking force by mixing 'ship-killing' weapons (such as the torpedo) and smaller ones (bombs less than 500lbs in size). At Taranto, more Swordfish carrying torpedoes could have caused even greater damage to the battle fleet, while damage inflicted by bomb-carrying aircraft was negligible. Had a planned follow-up raid taken place, it is a reasonable assumption that this lesson would have been absorbed, as it later was against *Tirpitz*.

Nevertheless, the damage caused by the striking force at Taranto was still out of all proportion to its size, and the losses suffered by the Swordfish aircrew. Additionally, the Regia Marina's losses were multiplied, as two battleships represented the limit of what dockyards could repair at once. This rendered *Conte di Cavour* an effective total loss, even though it was technically repairable.

The successes at Matapan and against *Bismarck* were more in line with expectations, but this required well-trained and experienced aircrews who were accustomed to working together as a unit under the command of a leader they understood. These criteria were not in place for the 1940 strike against *Scharnhorst* and the 1942 strike against *Tirpitz*, with the result that good opportunities were lost. The margin between excellent and poor results was fine.

Admiral Dudley Pound's fears for the survivability of fleet carriers in the Mediterranean proved to be close to the mark. *Ark Royal* and *Eagle* were sunk by submarines, while *Illustrious*, *Formidable* and *Indomitable* were all 'mission killed' by air attack and had to withdraw for serious repairs. Any fleet carrier operating for a sustained period in the Mediterranean between 1940 and 1943 was virtually guaranteed to receive heavy, even fatal damage at some point. This was a testament to the risk posed by torpedo-bombers – the Axis strained every sinew to knock carriers out – but it also limited their possibilities for success in the Mediterranean after 1941. After *Formidable*'s withdrawal, Fleet Air Arm torpedo-bombers enjoyed much success flying from Malta against merchant shipping, and in the Western Desert against the Afrika Korps, but there were few opportunities for attacks on Axis warships.

AXIS WARSHIPS

The torpedo hit that rendered *Bismarck* helpless has been called lucky, but the battleship's stern was an area of weakness that the Swordfish crews had been told would be vulnerable to a torpedo hit.

The vulnerability has often been attributed to the triple-shaft arrangement, but the shallow stern with long overhangs was a feature of all large Kriegsmarine warships, including the two-shaft Deutschland-class, and was adopted chiefly for its hydrodynamic properties. The shallow depth of the hull here reduced 'beam' strength and was vulnerable to shocks. The rudders were closer to the surface than on comparable designs, and consequently more liable to damage from torpedoes. The three-shaft arrangement was less efficient at steering with the screws than a four-shaft powertrain. All these factors meant that the damage caused by a torpedo hit in the stern would be worse, and the consequences of such damage more acute than on other contemporary battleships.

The common account of the torpedo hit on *Bismarck*'s stern understates its seriousness by emphasising only that the rudders jammed. In fact, the explosion caused the hull to 'whip', distorting the stern and weakening its attachment to the hull. The steering gear itself was protected by an armoured box, but this only added to the damage as it was more rigid than the structure around it, and could not flex with the hull. The resulting distortion jammed the rudder shafts, and made them impossible to fully free. When Dr. Robert Ballard discovered the wreck he confirmed that the stern had broken off, probably before the battleship sank.

Bismarck's failure to shoot down any Swordfish has been the subject of much debate and confusion over how such an ostensibly powerful ship could be hamstrung by obsolete biplanes, while failing to bring any of them down. Many factors contributed to this, including weather conditions, fatigue in the anti-aircraft gunners, poor design of the anti-aircraft systems and inferior equipment.

A popular theory suggests that *Bismarck*'s failure to down any Swordfish was an aberration, the battleship's fire-control being 'too modern' to account for the outdated aircraft. This theory is applied variously to the heavy anti-aircraft mountings or the directors. There is a grain of truth here, but in reality it had little or no effect. More influential factors were the design and execution of the system, and the conditions of the action.

A quad-20mm 2cm/65 C/38 'Vierling' light Flak battery on an unidentified Kriegsmarine warship during an exercise at Wilhelmshaven in 1940, showing the sight articulated by a pantograph from the gun itself. Kriegsmarine anti-aircraft gunners were initially well trained, although a lack of practice in service took its toll. (Author's Collection)

Bismarck's anti-aircraft fire-control was affected by a compromise between precision and the range of speeds across which it would effectively work. The wider the range of speeds that the director could accommodate, the poorer the precision at low speeds, as the difference between plotted positions became less distinguishable from 'noise' in the system.

Other factors, however, played a far greater role. *Bismarck* was only fitted with two of the correct, stabilised SL-8 directors, while the two aft positions were occupied by unstabilised EM-4M directors adapted from a land-based version as a stop gap. These were clearly inferior, less able to cope with rough conditions, and did not integrate well with the forward directors. There were also 'dead spots' not fully covered by a director. Furthermore, *Bismarck* was not fully fitted out with the newest mountings for the 10.5cm anti-aircraft guns – those forward were the older L/31 type, and aft mountings were the newer L/37. These had differences in cross-levelling, training and elevation speed. The newer mountings were paired with the inferior directors and the older mountings with the better directors, probably to partially offset the deficiencies in each, but that meant both fore and aft defences were flawed.

The 3.7cm guns were obsolete in 1941 and their performance was poor. They were also imperfectly situated, and *Bismarck's* captain noted the limited arcs of fire in some of these, and the 2cm guns, in October 1940. Furthermore, the director and gun crews had been at action stations for many hours in rough seas and cold conditions, and it is reasonable to expect that their efficiency would degrade over time. Even so, individual aircraft running in late, without the defences being split by multiple attacks, found it difficult or impossible to close to launch range. Gunfire was described in the report by *Ark Royal's* captain as 'Heavy and well directed . . . [the] impression is that fire control was split up into several groups of both large- and small-calibre guns, one group or more concentrating on individual aircraft' – a reasonably accurate assessment.

Kriegsmarine gunners were more successful during the attack on *Scharnhorst* on 20 June 1940 and on *Tirpitz* on 9 March 1942, with two torpedo-bombers being downed during each attack, and during the 'Channel Dash' on 12 February 1942. In the latter case it is difficult to assess how many of the six Swordfish might have been shot down by ship-based anti-aircraft rather than fighters, but the former probably contributed to the demise of two or three. More importantly, in all cases the attacking aircraft were prevented from scoring any hits.

The passive and active defences of Regia Marina warships against torpedo attack were relatively sophisticated, but in the right circumstances they were capable of being overwhelmed. The much-maligned Pugliese system actually worked relatively well, only failing badly in one case, although on two other notable occasions it was bypassed thanks to magnetically fired torpedoes.

At Taranto, the forwardmost hit on *Littorio* was outside the Pugliese system. The middle hit was in the forward part of the Pugliese system where the cylinder tapered, and therefore offered less protection than at the widest point, but it still contained the damage reasonably well. Flooding was a lot less severe as a result of this hit than the forward one. The hits to *Conte di Cavour* and *Duilio* were both beneath the hull, bypassing the Pugliese cylinders.

The only time a Pugliese cylinder was substantially overwhelmed was the hit on *Vittorio Veneto* at the Battle of Matapan. Here, the torpedo struck at the extreme aft end of the cylinder where it was only 60 per cent of the maximum diameter. German tests on the incomplete Littorio-class *Impero* revealed that detonation of 1,300lbs of TNT amidships did not cause the system to fail. In effect, the Pugliese system worked well where it was strongest, but hits outside its protection were liable to cause severe damage and flooding. That said, *Littorio* survived three torpedo hits at Taranto and *Vittorio Veneto* escaped at Matapan. Both ships were out of action for months, but lived to fight another day, unlike *Bismarck*.

Regia Marina anti-aircraft gunners were constrained in their training and practice by a lack of ammunition. In real-world conditions, however, they seem to have had similar levels of success to their Kriegsmarine counterparts. This is to say they occasionally brought down attacking aircraft and hindered others in their attacks, but were sometimes unable to prevent several significant losses.

According to a study by the Italian historian Enrico Cernuschi, German anti-aircraft weapons had a success rate of 4,553 projectiles fired per aircraft shot down, which fell to around 3,000 projectiles in 1943 after the introduction of radar-laid guns. British figures stand at 2,963 rounds-per-kill in February 1941, though estimates for Malta were around the 4,000 round mark. Italian anti-aircraft gunners in July 1943 recorded 3,707 rounds-per-kill when considering strictly confirmed results only. Few anti-aircraft guns were radar-laid. However, due to the shortage of ammunition, Italian gunners only fired around five per cent of the rounds expended by German anti-aircraft batteries. This should arguably have resulted in a much lower number of kills, while in similar circumstances, Italian anti-aircraft gunners actually downed comparable numbers of aircraft to their German counterparts.

The Swordfish from the first wave at Taranto that torpedoed *Conte di Cavour* was downed by gunners from that ship and the destroyer *Fulmine*, while an aircraft from the second wave was brought down by the cruiser *Gorizia* before it could launch an attack, according to some accounts blowing up in mid-air, and the

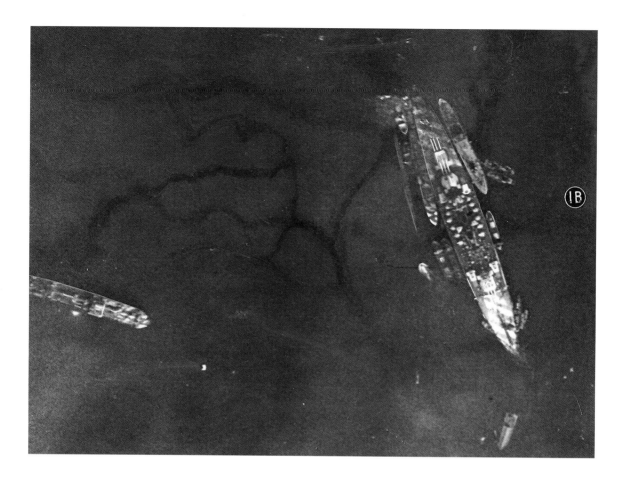

A retouched reconnaissance photograph issued to the press of the battleship *Littorio* after it had sustained three torpedo hits at Taranto in November 1940. The vessel's bow (uppermost) is awash and it is surrounded by support vessels. (Author's Collection)

Swordfish that attempted to torpedo *Vittorio Veneto* sustained damage but was able to recover to the parent carrier. These were likely victims of short-range anti-aircraft fire.

The anti-aircraft crew of *Duilio* told British observers after the Italian armistice that they could bring the guns into action within ten seconds of sighting the target, although this would depend on the accuracy of the ranges initially obtained. This was somewhat at odds with the experience of the torpedo-bombers at the Battle of Cape Spartivento, who found they were able to approach almost to the dropping point before being fired upon, and at the Battle of Calabria where aircrews reported relatively little anti-aircraft fire. Even at the Battle of Matapan, there was a notable delay before the anti-aircraft batteries opened up, although when they did they were effective, preventing some aircraft from attacking, and destroying one Albacore (albeit after it had launched its torpedo).

Training, experience and modifications to anti-aircraft batteries may have improved performance by the time of the Battle of Matapan, where incredibly dense defensive fire was reported, leading to some aircraft having to attack individually and opportunistically. The Albacore of Lt Cdr Dalyell-Stead, which torpedoed *Vittorio Veneto* during the second strike, was able to close to a distance estimated at 1,000m to drop its torpedo, but the biplane was shot down before it could escape. This was the only attacking aircraft lost to anti-aircraft fire.

AFTERMATH

From 1942, circumstances and strategic decision-making on both sides increasingly conspired to make engagements between Axis warships and Fleet Air Arm torpedo-bombers more and more unlikely. In the Mediterranean, occasional surface engagements took place, such as the Battles of Sirte and the action during the Operation *Harpoon* convoy, but no carriers were present. A lack of fuel hampered Regia Marina operations, and the Royal Navy had no carrier based at Alexandria between May 1941 and April 1943.

The Italian command hoped Japan's entry into the war would cause the British to weaken the Mediterranean Fleet, but the Royal Navy maintained enough strength to prevent Italian domination. Nevertheless, the Regia Marina was able to provide battleship escorts to North African convoys, with most of the supplies getting through.

Following *Formidable*'s withdrawal after it was heavily bombed during the evacuation of Crete in May 1941, the Fleet Air Arm's torpedo-bomber presence in the eastern Mediterranean was restricted to disembarked squadrons. These were divided between Malta, including 828 and 830 NASs, and North Africa, including 815 NAS, all operating a mix of Albacores and Swordfish. Those squadrons in the Western Desert were seconded to the RAF, and they made a name for themselves target marking and carrying out night attacks on Axis forces. The units only engaged in anti-shipping work when it did not conflict with their

Kriegsmarine warships at anchor in a Norwegian fjord – an increasingly commonplace occurrence in the second half of the war. To the left is the cruiser *Admiral Hipper* and in the centre, distant, the battleship *Scharnhorst*. (Author's Collection)

The chief Fleet Air Arm strike aircraft in the Pacific was the Avenger, seen here over US warships. The majority of its targets were land-based. The Avenger/Tarpon only attempted one torpedo strike in British service, and the aircrew involved failed to locate the target. (Author's Collection)

army support responsibilities. The squadrons on Malta were chiefly employed in night attacks on Axis convoys when fuel and serviceability allowed.

A fleet carrier was not permanently based in the eastern Mediterranean again until *Formidable* returned in April 1943, shortly before the final defeat of Axis forces in North Africa.

Fleet carriers had returned in force to the western Mediterranean in the second half of 1942 in support of two large Malta convoys and then the invasion of French North Africa. Albacore squadrons supported the latter, but the expected intervention of Axis naval forces did not take place.

In northern waters, after the failed attack on *Tirpitz* in March 1942, *Victorious* continued to escort Russian convoys until the summer. However, there was no contact with Kriegsmarine warships. In August, the carrier was temporarily assigned to the Mediterranean for the Malta convoy Operation *Pedestal*. Afterwards, it returned to Britain for a refit, and the ship was out of circulation until November, then operated with the US Navy in the Pacific in 1943, not returning until September. The Home Fleet's carrier forces, now equipped with Barracudas in place of the old biplane torpedo-bombers, began to operate with confidence and increasing skill, with raids against *Tirpitz* and shipping along the Norwegian coast. However, the torpedo was no longer their chief weapon, dive-bombing being the preferred method of attack.

After the IJN's Indian Ocean raid in April 1942, the Royal Navy avoided contact with Japanese naval forces unless under advantageous conditions. The carriers *Indomitable* and *Illustrious* were involved in the invasion of Madagascar in May 1942, where Swordfish carried out their last torpedo attacks on surface warships with a strike on a Vichy French gunboat and auxiliary cruiser.

When the Royal Navy's carrier force gained the strength to move back east, first in the East Indies and then into the Pacific, its role was overwhelmingly against land targets. Barracudas were initially the aircraft of choice, replaced from mid-1944 with Avengers as the more appropriate aircraft for this type of operations. This essentially meant an end to any chance of the Fleet Air Arm repeating its 1940–41 successes in torpedo attacks against Axis warships.

In truth, the chances of such exploits being repeated had begun to diminish – a fact that was apparent even in mid-1941. Major warships' anti-aircraft defences were continually strengthened, with more and better guns, improvements in fire control, and radar. The weaknesses that allowed a force of relatively low-performance aircraft to close to torpedo range were steadily eradicated. The US Navy proved in 1944–45 that torpedo-bombers were still highly effective against even the largest warships as long as overwhelming numbers of aircraft were available – something the Fleet Air Arm could not replicate until the final months of the war, by which time there were few major Axis warships left afloat.

FURTHER READING

PUBLISHED WORKS

Bagnasco, Erminio and de Toro, Augusto, Italian Battleships – Conte di Cavour and Duilio Classes 1911–1956 (Seaforth, 2021)

Bagnasco, Erminio and de Toro, Augusto, *The Littorio Class – Italy's Last and Largest Battleships 1937–1948* (Seaforth, 2011)

Campbell, John, *Naval Weapons of World War Two* (Naval Institute Press, 1985)

Dannreuther, Raymond, *Somerville's Force H* (Aurum, 2005)

Friedman, Norman, *Naval Anti-Aircraft Guns and Gunnery* (Seaforth, 2013)

Jones, Ben, *The Fleet Air Arm in the Second World War, Volumes 1 and 2* (Routledge, 2016 and 2018)

Koszela, Witold, *Battleships of the III Reich Volumes 1 and 2*, (MMP Books, 2018)

Mearns, David and White, Rob, *Hood and Bismarck – The Deep-Sea Discovery of an Epic Battle* (Channel 4, 2001)

Wragg, Davis, *Swordfish – The Story of the Taranto Raid* (Cassell, 2003)

WEBSITES

Armoured Carriers – Armoured flight deck aircraft carrier action and damage reports 1940–1945 at www.armouredcarriers.com

Crusader Project – the Axis and Commonwealth perspectives of the Winterschlacht (Winter Battle) in North Africa, November 1941 to February 1942 at rommelsriposte.com

Drachinifel Naval Historiographer YouTube channel at www.youtube.com/c/Drachinifel

German Battleship Bismarck, Interrogation of Survivors, Naval Intelligence Division, August, 1941 at www.uboatarchive.net/Int/BismarckINT.htm

International Naval Research Organization, Bismarck's Final Battle, William H. Garzke Jr and Robert O. Dulin Jr at www.navweaps.com/index_inro/INRO_Bismarck.php

HMS Glorious – The cover up of Churchill's Operation *Paul* at www.hmsglorious.com

Garzke Jr and Robert O. Dulin Jr at www.navweaps.com/index_inro/INRO_Bismarck.php

Naval History Live YouTube channel at www.youtube.com/DrAlexanderClarke

RECOMMENDED TWITTER FEEDS

Comando Supremo – Italy in WW2 @comando_supremo

Italian Military Archives @ITM_archives

Marcus Faulkner @NavalHistWar

Matt Warwick @mpwarwick

Naval Historian (Dr Phil Weir) @navalhistorian

Navy General Board @thegeneralboard

INDEX